Formation of the Missing Man (Where Man Becomes Missing from God)
Copyright © 2015 by Ernest T. Davis II. All rights reserved.

No part of this publication may be reproduced, stored in a retrieval system or transmitted in any way by any means, electronic, mechanical, photocopy, recording or otherwise without the prior permission of the author except as provided by USA copyright law.

This book is designed to provide accurate and authoritative information with regard to the subject matter covered. This information is given with the understanding that the author is engaged in rendering legal or professional advice. Since the details of your situation are fact dependent, you should additionally seek the services of a competent professional.

Published by Ernest T. Davis II

Book design copyright © 2015 by Ernest T. Davis II

Cover design by Kevin J. Bright
Image copyright is held by Mark Wiley, 221 Central Park Ave, Wilmette, IL 60091
TITLE OF IMAGE: *Then the Lord God Formed Man from the Clay Of The Earth*

ISBN: 978-0-9964988-0-7
Religion/Christian Life/Devotional
June 9, 2015

A very special place in my heart is reserved for Colonel George B. Fomundam. He is the missing man in this formation having gone to glory. I dedicate this to his influence. His love and wisdom lives on in me. To God be the glory for his assignment on earth.

Endorsements

'Formation of the Missing Man' is a contribution that could only be made by a man - and Dr. Ernest Davis is the man chosen by God to address this serious issue. While women and children also suffer because of 'missing men', the recognition of men's plight by another man lends greater validity to the work. With candor and humility, Dr. Davis seeks to be an obedient vessel, encouraging men to confront what he himself has had to face. He is not only transparent about his journey as a 'missing man', but he also provides meaningful reflection exercises to guide readers toward healing.

Rev. Esi M. Mathis
Family Justice Advocate & Soros Justice Fellow
The Campaign for the Fair Sentencing of Youth
(Daughter of a missing man)

Dr. Ernest T. Davis II, look what God has done in you. I'm extremely proud of you and honored that you'd afford me an opportunity to endorse this latest project. This is an honor that a kid growing up in Northwest Washington, D. C. never imagined concerning us both. God is truly grand and worthy of more praise than I can ever give Him alone.

Many people know you (Ernest) today from your ministry, guidance, counseling or other extremely positive encounters. I am truly blessed to know from where God has brought you (Tony and to many "T-Shirt") and I (Capt'n). To that I say, thank you Lord. May this heartfelt expression you've put into print be an influential blessing to readers of all ages, sexes, origins and nationalities, but especially men! May God continue to work on us both my Brother in Christ and from the old neighborhood. What an amazing journey you've traveled, from jumping out of High School to jumping out of airplanes while serving your country in the United States Army to taking giant leaps for Jesus.

Thank you Dr. Ernest (Tony) Davis for the opportunity to share in your blessing; I'm honored.

CURTIS A. JENNINGS
Chief Master Sergeant (Retired)
30 Years United States Air Force
Lifelong Childhood Friend

Formation of the Missing Man

(Where Man Becomes Missing from God)

Dr. Ernest T. Davis II, Th.D.

"Our best response to His adjustment is to cooperate".

Pastor Anthony W. Wallace

Contents

Dedication

Acknowledgements

Introduction

The remainder of this work will be a continuous musing that will not have chapter numbers. At the end of each section there are three questions for reflection and discussion. Find a brother with whom you can become totally transparent; naked. The desire is that it will be a continual draw for more people and thereby creating more reflection. Understandably, this is not the literary norm for many including myself although I have used it once before on a previous work (*Musings of the World's Fool)*. However, upon instruction of the Holy Spirit my obedience is tantamount to my love of God and thereby the anointing in His instruction. Just in me writing this is thinking outside the proverbial box; even for myself. Therefore, I am in expectation of a blessing for the reader that cannot be contained that may bestowed upon others for their blessing. Whisper to your spirit; "I will allow God to adjust my life by any means necessary". We will never embrace manhood until we embrace our fragility as a man. We are more fragile than we think.

Dedication

This is dedicated to all men who ponder what truly manhood is and whether God's true intention was missed. To the women of our lives who desire the God-given description of manhood. He will give you the inner peace to trust Him as we develop. To my sons both natural and spiritual in this earth, I salute and encourage you. The only delay in becoming a man is not allowing a father to impart into the sons. As I was out of position through ignorance and generational ignorance, I am now in position through lineage and adopted lineage. The expectation is that wisdom must be imparted.

Kenneth A. Davis, I miss you man! He was my brother and at times confidant who could not bear what was revealed to him concerning our lives and origin. He has left this realm. But, my love and honor for him continues. We went from hellions doing many unspeakable things under the sun to sitting in a church on each side of our mother worshipping; voluntarily! God blessed me with the time I had with you. I am glad that I took each moment in the month before your transition to speak, pray and cry with you. My joy is that you are now in the presence of the fullness of joy.

Certainly I cannot be remiss in not dedicating this as well to Mrs. Barbara Flowers. She is a powerful woman of God who would actually pray for us while in Roosevelt High School in Washington, DC. Her determination to ensure that we had hope and direction produced so many men and women of God until I call her to thank her. Her sorority, Delta Sigma Theta, possessed a gem in her! She would actually come get me out of a craps game and make me come to English class. It always seems as if she knew when I was winning and showed up. There is a place in my heart for her eternally. I sat one day for hours and pondered how God loved me so much to place such people in my life to guide me and challenge me. It blew my mind. And, to be brutally honest she was the only teacher in my latter high school years (more like two years of skipping school) that made such an impact on me until I would pick up a pen later to use as a tool of catharsis; releasing pain and pleasure.

Dedicated to the memory of Richard (Richie) McNeil, my brother-in-law who became a brother and father surrogate without even knowing the impact he placed on my life to continue on. Your life and wisdom gave me life and direction even in the midst of familial dysfunction and pain. And now, I incorporate that wisdom in my release to other men. I pour a snifter of Remy Martin Louis XIII Black Pearl Limited Edition on the ground in your honor; the finest cognac known! The imparted wisdom is worth infinitely more than this.

Acknowledgements

My Lord and Savior, Jesus Christ Who is the epitome of manhood in that He truly gave Himself for His Bride, the church, nurturing us that He may present us spotless and without blemish.

Lady Davis who has taught and allowed me to love the way Christ loved me. A man cannot find a virtuous woman as related in Proverbs 31. She must be presented just as Eve was presented to Adam after she has already been in His presence. Yet it is the man's responsibility and freedom to choose who is to be his help meet and allow her to function as intended. It is up to the man to recognize the value far beyond rubies and precious stones in his presence even if it is hidden.

With much love I acknowledge Pastors and Apostles Anthony and Margo Wallace who shepherd and develop sons in the Gospel, not church members. I speak Apostleship because they have both had personal encounters with the risen Jesus. Both have a special message for the Body of Christ with a voice to the region. They are both recognized among others as those that are apostolic; laying proper foundation. Yet, they are not concerned with titles as long as they have function. They both have a 'grill presentation' even though you may be sitting in the back of the church. I have looked around and many including myself had that look of correction and direction. One can never be the same under the anointed and directed teaching of the Holy Spirit through positioned people of God.

I warmly acknowledge Pastor Marvin Wilson. This man loved me to life. Even in times when I wanted him to go take a flying leap and pretty much said so. He was consistent with agape love in my sloppy life. Sometimes just to be available to the wounded will bring supernatural healing without even a word being spoken. I am grateful beyond description to the artistic eye of Mark Wiley for his captured image; *Then the Lord God formed man from the clay of the earth.* Such skill and talent enabled the cover for this book to be formed.
In addition, the artist of design *Kevin Bright* is an awesome man for such an undertaking. He painstakingly put this together to capture the essence of the book. Simply, AWESOME.

Introduction

Man. The term seems to be a cut and dried word and concept, yet possessing many facets. However, in this age, there is nothing cut and dried about manhood according to modern culture. Misconceptions range from attire, to employment, to sexual prowess to control. However, there is nothing more flawed than what society tells us a man should be. We look in the media to see what is presented to us; often the most ludicrous examples of a warped and profitable mind. If we have no inkling of our true purpose we will buy into this farce. Then we look toward society and familial norms to be the benchmark for manhood only to discover that gender neutrality has become the norm erasing any masculine boundaries including the paternal pattern for God with His Son. Far too often we are only perpetuating the same mistakes and shortcomings that have haunted us for generations; the hodgepodge of manly misconceptions even perpetuated by the Church at times. For, there can be no man without a woman and not in the same body. And, these shortcomings are nothing more than a deviation from what God has instructed us from the very beginning. It is terrible how we can look to everyone else for direction except to Him that gave direction before the foundation of the world.

We must return to the foundation and original concept for manhood as recorded in the Word of God; the Bible. God is the only One able and qualified to dictate what we are to be as men, for He created us in His image. Since this direction is often negated from the same society that wishes to discredit God as sovereign and alive, then it will take those of us who are called to proclaim the truth as it is. Is this a popular message? Not in any aspect of our present society. But, then again what is a popular message when you go against what fallen human nature wants; soulish desires?

Once we return to the original concept, we see how far we have erred from the truth. Somehow we thought that our examples of manhood that were not fashioned in the manner God intended were more reliable and secure. And yet, I cannot place blame completely on the man because there are many that rejected the godly example given. I must allow this to be shared by all in society and familial order. But, in honesty, we can't reach our intended potential with social and carnal mentalities coupled with generations old errors. They may feel good and even be sufficient for a time according to societal culture. But, only if we understand this sufficiency is restricting and crippling men at best.

As we travel through this lifetime, we need to beware that we carry this ill-fated legacy with us; unknowingly passing it on to our offspring of both genders. Our sons, if they have seen this deviation, begin to think that this must be correct because my father lived it. Or even worse, sons think they have their own answers because there was no father figure or one that was scandalized either through action or word to emulate. Very possibly the father was absent, restricted or just not involved. Or, the father was hindered from involvement by many factors. Our daughters begin searching for the same type of man portrayed by their father.

WHY ME?

Of all men in this world, why me Lord? I asked this question one night as I was wrestling in the bed after a day of spiritual failure. I had recapitulated my day and the shortcomings even into the evening prior to me attempting sleep. I went over in my mind the Word as God spoke it. I was to confess or agree with Him that I had sinned and He would faithfully forgive me and cleanse me from all unrighteousness. Just the meditation on that one Scripture (1 John 1:9) had me in awe at such a God that I serve. His Son paid the price in advance; well before the foundation of the world. All, I had to do was agree 12with Him that I had blown it that day and He did the rest. This did not give me the right to continuously go looking to fall short, but if I did God had already provided what was needed to remove all guilt from me

I especially was wrestling with things that connected me to childhood.

Yet, that wasn't enough. I was just beginning to settle in on that truth when all of a sudden Daddy began speaking to me. He wanted me to continue writing and get this work out to men: another musing! Well, I thought for a second then began speaking. Didn't He know I just came to Him saying how I had blown it? I especially was wrestling with things that connected me to childhood. Words my mother had spoken began to creep back into my mind forming a stronghold. And, now God tells me to "do this" and keep it moving. I wanted to stay right there. I wanted to not move because of spoken unworthiness of anything in life from my family and others had resurfaced. I wanted to wallow in the mud of abusive words spoken in times past. It was actually getting comfortable as I began to recap again all that I had blown that day. Yet, He gently said to move on and complete the assignment I was given. Well, so much for my pity party. He crashed it and put me back on the street. After all, He had cleansed me so I had no right to demand filthiness.

We are the ones that know we don't have it all together and are totally dependent on Him and His promises to us.

That very same question is that many men will ask of God in varying ways. Why me? He said "you" because then no one can say it was of you! A self-righteous man will boast and brag even before the task is completed. He will think and at least attempt to portray that it was under his own power, skill and ability that something was accomplished. God would never get the glory with such a person. They would already have the glory claimed before the onset of the task! Therefore, He comes and finds us, the ones that have our head down in sorrow that we have failed Him. We are the ones that know we don't have it all together and are totally dependent on Him and His promises to us. We are those that He calls to use. But, we still ask the same question; why me? God is calling those that may not come to the house of worship to be His voice in places and arenas that religious people dare go for fear of looking impious.

The athletes that are adored so very much on the border of being worshipped often have disconnections because of their fame.

After about ten minutes of whining with no answer, I conceded and attempted to go to sleep. I remember asking Him to speak to me in my sleep; in dreams. Well, I don't know if I ever truly got to sleep. I do know that I was flooded with things that were of Him. These were things that He is doing. He is calling men from the most unlikely places for the most unlikely tasks. We can look at an alcoholic or addict and deduct that there is a shortcoming. We can look at one with a variant sexual identity to conclude that there is a need for God's hand. Yet, we can't look at the CEO of a Fortune 500 company and see there is a deficit of relationship to God. We won't dare look at our own President of the United States and see that there is a disconnection from the God of Abraham, Isaac and Jacob; the God of the Founding Fathers. The athletes that are adored so very much on the border of being worshipped often have disconnections because of their fame. Therefore, God is calling those that may not come to the house of worship to be His voice in places and arenas that religious people dare go for fear of looking impious.

Imagine if someone saw you sitting in a sports bar regardless of what was occurring. What would they think? What if they saw you coming out of a known drug den? How about possibly the back door of a strip bar? All of these places would cause a murmur. Yet, in every one of these locations there are souls needing to hear the Gospel in order for the seed to be planted in their lives. Are we so callous to think that another person will be the one to go there?

There was a darkness that had begun to take up residence over the region of the city.

Two instances come to mind in thinking of why me. One is with a man that I know in ministry; Pastor Ricky Bright. As a young minister he has always had a burning for the disenfranchised. He approached me, at the time very urban in nature, to help him find a certain woman he had been ministering to in his workplace. The word was that she had returned to prostitution and drug use. I told him that if she didn't want to be found she could stay hidden since he had the urban demeanor of a choir boy in a rap concert. At that time he had no street smarts whatsoever! He begged me to take him there. During the day another person had been shot and killed in a sandwich shop which was on the edge of the "strip". Therefore the spiritual climate was very tense in the area. There was a darkness that had begun to take up residence over the region of the city. I told him to walk beside me and just be quiet.

I am sure her vocabulary would have never made the church bulletin or the Sunday Women's Tea.

We were approached by a thug that wanted to challenge us. I stood firm knowing the implications of backing down especially in the area we were along with what had occurred that day. I looked and he was behind me! I really tore into him explaining that he should never do that no matter how scared he was! We continued around the corner. I told him I would put his request on the "bulletin board". He took the urban vernacular as meaning a literal bulletin board! What I meant was that I would put the word out on the street and we would find her as long as it was me and not him that asked. Well, not even five minutes later in turning the corner she bumped into me. I told her that I had a friend looking for her. When she inquired who it was I presented Ricky. She was not happy at all seeing him and made it known in a verbal and abusive manner. I am sure her vocabulary would have never made the church bulletin or the Sunday Women's Tea. He never understood how I could do in less than thirty minutes which included travel time to and from along with the encounter and he couldn't do it all day. This is one instance of the answer to the "why me?" question.

He would go to the club that he had at one time frequented and ask if anyone needed prayer before they left.

The next instance is one of a young minister named Daniel Gueh who shared part of his testimony. He is from an area of New Jersey known for crime, drugs and violence. When he received the Lord, he told me that he actually went back to the same liquor store that he would buy his alcohol from, standing out front to witness and minister. In addition, he would go to the club that he had at one time frequented and ask if anyone needed prayer before they left. God calls many who are truly not the norm. There is an innate desire to rescue those of places and people of whom we frequented. It makes no sense. We all experience it.

Now, after being up well before sunrise to ensure I captured all of the impartation of the Holy Spirit, I understand why God would not answer my selfish and horribly cowardly question. Now the question is why not me. I have been damaged; abused and neglected enough to ensure that even if I wanted to take the glory, no one would give it to someone like the "me" they perceive! So, my brothers please don't waste your time in bargaining or asking silly questions of God. Just handle the assignment. Selah.

Reflection

Why do you think God chose you?

How do you see yourself?

How did you see yourself?

Formation of This Missing Man

The hardest thing for any man to do is to look at himself honestly and grasp the concept of being missing from the formation of God. Adam did it. He never acknowledge that He was missing from God; alas God's question of his location. We do it on a daily basis if not careful. I had done this for years before understanding the importance of repentance and even the allowance of things to die in my life which included many things that I loved dearly. Yet, we lean toward the group connection when God may be calling us to another more intimate formation.

I could not ask or answer the proverbial "compared to what" question.

My personal failure to meet the various formations of God began as a youth. Examples that I saw were not the examples of God for me. While there were examples present close by, I could not discern their authenticity because I didn't know an authentic example. I could not ask or answer the proverbial "compared to what" question. I only could compare my accountability to what I had observed from life. Therefore, I was destined to go through a period of cleansing that lasted about forty years. I'm glad the Lord loved me enough to allow this. I'm eternally grateful.

My non-accountability for the formations of life began with youthful upbringing and familial life. Much abuse of many forms caused an angry spirit coupled by low self-esteem. Even in these instances it was all used for God's glory! While the anger was used as a fuel to defend that which was perceived as right, the low self-esteem allowed me to find escape in reading which has served me well to this very day. Reading is an action that many men don't do either by refusal or not understanding the need to do such. I can recall my desire to read transforming me from the residence or streets of Washington, DC to exotic places or fictional existences. This was in order to get away to a place of slight rejuvenation in order to return and go through the valley of dysfunction. I had no idea what this was until I chose to seek guidance concerning all of these emotions, actions and behaviors.

Those that were in the church could not understand how to minister to me either by their ignorance or my refusal to disclose truth out of mistrust for their intentions.

God was so gracious that He gently guided me to counselors of Christian natures. All were placed strategically in society to touch people in ministry that was their paid vocation. This is why we need to train disciples to operate outside of the church instead of competing inside of the church. There will be those who must minister in the churches. However, the vast majority of "need" is outside the doors and may never come in the doors. This was the case with me. Those that were in the church could not understand how to minister to me either by their ignorance or my refusal to disclose truth out of mistrust for their intentions. By the way, there can be a misguided and misused trust that exists in religious circles. Yet, God placed me in circles of spiritual people; one even being a Muslim that later converted to Christianity.

Then there was my initial meltdown with the streets. I was trying so very hard to fit in until I had become somewhat ruthless in what I would do in order to be accepted. Deep inside, I knew this was wrong. Yet, the need to belong is so strong until a person will override the righteous awareness in them given by God. The need to belong is a strong attraction and often if not checked moves toward the wrong connection. Yet, God even used this to begin my transformation by joining the military. Why? My rationale was if I was going to be shot at I may as well be paid for the danger.

Initially, there was no patriotic foundation, only an economic one. The same desire to belong and be reimbursed for membership followed me into the military. Even there I could belong and go to great lengths to be accepted. This led to membership in specific units of prestige. Did I do it for patriotism? No. Yet, along the way I developed a love for my country that remains to this day. But, first I had to embrace the dollar to see the mindset; in God we trust. Then I began to trust God slowly, but surely.

While still embracing the pain which also was accompanied by fear and anger it required additional pain to be placed on me.

My military career was marked by many, many instances of mistakes and behavior that was not conducive to godly living. But, because of the development that was taking place, I was being gently guided even through chastisement into a place in God that was awesome. While still embracing the pain which also was accompanied by fear and anger it required additional pain to be placed on me. This was in order to fill up that pain container so full that I had fear of it consuming me and anger that I had all the pain that was not released. Then I began to seek help.

All of these people were instrumental in the process outlined by Apostle Nate Holcomb; face it, trace it, erase it and replace it.

But, as an onion has many layers, so does your healing and deliverance. It doesn't come at one time, but in increments. If God allowed all of that to be done in me it would have killed me surely. He allowed things to be taken and replaced in me. There were those who spoke life to me. There were those who walked beside me. There were those who chastised me. And, there were those who did nothing but not condemn me. All of these people were instrumental in the process outlined by Apostle Nate Holcomb; face it, trace it, erase it and replace it. This is an ongoing process.

I had a Goliath in my life.

Even in the course of life there is a continuous searching for God in the situations and existence. It never ends. I often use the analogy of Goliath. The name Goliath at its Hebraic root means uncovered. While the suffix assigned to the root word adds the meaning of "splendor" to the proper noun or name, the root of this "splendor" will be an uncovered display of existence (*golyath*) (גליית) Yet, if we take the suffix of (ת) away while leaving the root (*galah)* (גלי) we still have the foundation of uncovered. And, I was truly uncovered; naked!!! I had a Goliath in my life. And, he was taunting me!

Don't despise your God-sent help because it didn't arrive in the package you envisioned.

But, praises be to God that five smooth stones were given to me. One was for the immediate annihilation of Goliath. The other four were for his brothers that would surface in my desire to become accounted for in the Kingdom of God. They will defy you just as Goliath did. A reference to the brothers that were eventually slain is recorded in 2 Samuel 21:18-22. I can point to the Goliath in my life as well as the four brothers that had to be slain in order for me to be free. And, all of them were slain with rocks; symbolic of Christ. All of them had to be slain at different times, not immediately as was Goliath. Perhaps this is the key to understanding the "why" of how long our struggles are. And, to this day, I am free from the opinions and need for acceptance of others. Yet, I must remain in a constant humility in order to understand that it was God who preserved and delivered me from myself. But, I offer a word of caution. Don't despise your God-sent help because it didn't arrive in the package you envisioned.

It takes the understanding of the painful change in order to change the painful.

The most painful yet rewarding adjustment, correction and instruction came in the house of God. It is here where imperfect people practice imperfect practices with perfect intentions. This often leads to pain with intentions to create healing. Yet, in all of this we grow. It takes the understanding of the painful change in order to change the painful. So, while this is but a smidgen in this present section of where I began missing my formation, it will be enough to begin the search on how men in general miss theirs. The first person you must be honest with is the one in the mirror. He must be measured by the Word of God, not the words of other flawed men.

Reflection

What began your missing formation?

How did you "recover" and begin to be accountable? What Goliath did you have to slay?

Can you see how the pain has actually been necessary for your healing?

Men Tend To Believe With the Wrong Faith

Immediately when I begin speaking to men, there comes to mind something that is telling us as men what we are doing wrong things. Someone is always telling us what we are doing wrong. Now, here I am telling us what we are doing wrong. Could it be that we are not technically doing anything wrong, but doing it the wrong way? Could it be that we are not doing something wrong, but we are not doing something right either? Such is the case with our faith.

I personally love to dig into the Word of God for His nuggets hidden in plain view. I can take a verse and go off on so many rabbit trails from words, sentence arrangement, word order and a myriad of other things. There will be so many rabbit trails until my notes will look like a bunch of words and phrases at varying angles on the paper! Therefore, I am not filled with kicks and giggles when the sermon is preached and I walk away from the worship service feeling that I have it all together.

A lot can be wrong with my faith in God if I use it at the wrong time.

At times, I feel that I am the only one that needs to go back and ponder what I just heard. I must go and meditate on this word given; let it sink down into my inner being. I guess it's that all or nothing mentality that we often have as men that arises. So, with no disrespect to the preacher, pastor or evangelist but I must be a Berean. I must first of all go and see if this is true in context which it was preached. Then I will go to my little area of earth that I have assigned to be just for God and me. No one else is welcomed there in my assigned moment unless they will join in with God speaking to me and the worship of God. So why do I do this? I do it because of my faith in God. What can be wrong with my faith in God? A lot can be wrong with my faith in God if I use it at the wrong time. Now, I know you are wondering how you can use faith in God "at the wrong time". I'm glad you asked even though your facial demeanor is one of utter confusion.

I once heard someone speak how they wanted to go find the devil's house and kick his door down to fight with him. Dumb.

What we do wrong is appropriate a "saying" or "cliché" from the Bible and run with it. So often instead of proper exegesis we rely on what we have heard which came from someone who heard it, who heard it from still yet another person. So, in essence too often what we are operating from is a watered down religious cliché void of power and even common sense. I once heard someone speak how they wanted to go find the devil's house and kick his door down to fight with him. Dumb. This is just plain dumber than a bag of rocks. I don't say it to ridicule the person, but to challenge the leadership responsible for teaching the Word of God in practical application. First of all, if the devil had and abode with a door that we could access, I don't think you could kick the door down. Next, even Michael the Archangel didn't contend with the devil, but said the Lord rebuke thee. So, what makes us feel that we have big feet capable of bringing his door to be inoperable? Just do the will of God and the enemy will find you! Trust me when I state emphatically that the enemy will send a representative to you informing you that he is trying to kick your door down!

So, what kind of faith am I speaking of? There is a faith in God and a faith "of" God. I continuously hear people quote Mark 11. I purposely don't give verses much forcing the reader to search out the passage. Far too often we go straight to one verse and make a doctrine on it instead of studying the verse in context. Therefore, I purposely at times will not give a specific verse opting to give a complete chapter instead, and even possibly just the book!

In Mark 11 we often hear to have faith in God. If we have faith in God then we can tell the mountain to move and it would go fling itself into the sea. So, depending on how we mentally process a spiritual treasure, we may just stop there. For many years I stumbled on this and actually became very disheartened concerning it. A well-meaning pastor continued to tell me that my faith "in" God was not strong enough. I was told that I needed more faith "in" God to speak to the mountain. As a young Christian (and even as an older one) I continually asked God to give me more faith. I had no idea of other parts of the Bible that spoke of God giving us "the" measure of faith; the same measure of total faith. I had no idea that I was asking amiss!

I wasn't good enough to search the Scriptures according to my spiritual parental figure.

I then (with my analytical mind) began to think that if what he said was true then everyone needed different levels of faith to be saved by grace! Now, my mind (soul) was really thrown out in left field. So, I went back to him and began to present my reasoning. Then I was ridiculed and told that I was letting the devil use me. How? Wasn't I just told that I needed more faith? So, that would lead me to believe that God had on his faith supply shelf more little packages with varying amounts of faith; of which I must have received the wrong package for my dilemma! We can wound young saints with our ancestral generational clichés. So, here I am again going out of the church with the same wounds that the world inflicted driving me into the sanctuary; wounds on my self-esteem and intelligence. I wasn't good enough to search the Scriptures according to my spiritual parental figure. So upon keeping a measure of faith to continually cry to God, I was able to hold on (after falling times too numerous to count) until He gave me a nugget. I was told to look into the language in which the Gospel was written; Greek. What I discovered was that I had the wrong faith! I was having faith "in" God instead of the faith "of" God! I had my faith in God trying to do the work of the faith "of" God where He was responsible for doing the work!

Jesus took this for a training moment to let them know what they must have in the very near future.

In Mark 11 Jesus was instructed the disciples to secure the colt and ass needed for a triumphal ride into the holy city of Jerusalem. He passed a fig tree that didn't have the fruit for the season that it was to have. So, Jesus cursed the fig tree and kept walking on His mission. The next day as they passed the tree the disciples noticed that it was dead. They were amazed. Jesus took this for a training moment to let them know what they must have in the very near future. He said that they were to have faith (wait for it) OF God. I understand that the King James Version reads to have faith "in" God. But, we must realize that English is a bastardized language; constantly growing daily while having the roots of our words in other cultures. So, here lies the dilemma for men.

The word "theou" directs our faith to be God's faith.

We have been having faith in God when as the original Greek records that Christ said to have the faith "of" God. The word "*theou*" directs our faith to be God's faith. Now, how does one have the faith "of" God? We don't. We just have the faith in God that He will operate in His own faith to do what He says. So, here's the brain cell smasher. God has faith in Himself concerning Himself. He needs not have faith in any other person, place or thing because He is all in all. So, when God says something it is inconceivable for Him to think in any minute fashion that it will not come true. Before He even speaks He already knows it to be true; period. It has already happened in His mind; like we could ever measure or know how His mind operates. So, Jesus said have the faith "of" God according to the Greek manuscripts.

In order to have the faith of God, you must first have faith in God.

As you continue reading in the pericope, He spoke to the tree and kept walking. He didn't stop to see if it would obey. He just kept walking. Why? Because the faith of God, one doesn't need an audience if you truly have His faith that is operating. It's not your faith. It's God's faith.

A good example would be if we compared ourselves to God in telling someone to do something. I know this may be sacrilegious to some. But, get over it. We are in no way equating ourselves to be God, only using this as a viable and simplistic example. Say if God spoke for the lawn to be mowed. He would never come back to check to see if it was completed. It was because God's faith demanded and performed that the lawn was to be mowed; period. God spoke, "Lawn be mowed". And, it was mowed. Yet, if we spoke the same thing, we would have to "see" it mowed before it could produce faith. Why is this so? Because God's word can never return to Him void. Our word can return to us without accomplishing what we sent it out to accomplish. So, the faith in this situation is of God not in God.

It is God's faith that moved the mountain; not our faith in God.

Again, I have faith in God. So when I speak to the fig trees of my life I need to have the faith of God that it will be done. But, I caution you. In order to have the faith of God, you must first have faith in God. You cannot have this faith in God without obedience which involves accepting his Son Jesus. Without going through the Son, you will never access the Father in order to have His faith. It is then that we can say that we are one with the Father. It is then that all that He has becomes all that we have which includes the faith of God. Then we are relieved of us not having the faith to move the mountain. Why? It is God's faith that moved the mountain; not our faith in God. That's why! Men, we are now free to allow the mountains of life to be moved because it's not by our faith that we move them. Daddy's faith moves the mountains. It's just up to us to keep walking while having faith in Him.

Reflection

What has been an aspect of wrong faith that you remember?

What was the corrective action?

How do you define and explain experiential faith vs. experimental faith?

The Bait of Scars

As little boys we are always falling getting scarred. Even in adult life by the nature of our gender we engage in activities that can cause scarring. Reckless living is not limited to young men. Often older men begin to have crisis and may engage in reckless behavior as well. So, we are collectors of scars. The problem is we hide them instead of putting them on display. We will cover them with garments, tattoos, or just hide them to keep them from inquiring eyes. Perhaps God wishes for us to display the scars to draw others to His Kingdom. They are like beacons of light. It draws people to us. What we may see as a painful experience may be the port of comfort for another to know that here is a port of where I can dock my ship of confusion.

We as men still cringe if someone touches our "boo-boo".

In my personal life I bear about the scars on my arm from going through a glass door that was reinforced with wire in high school. The circumstances surrounding my going through that door can be discussed and debated with many having opinions, thoughts memories or reasons. Either way my scars are there and I went through the door causing the pain. They attract quite a bit of attention when displayed as one would imagine. Pastor Anthony Wallace gives instructions concerning our scars; don't hide them. He encourages us to use them to give a testimony. The scar means that healing has occurred. Otherwise there would still be a scab with the possibility of it bleeding again. Yet, with the scar tissue, the wound has healed. And, in most cases the scar tissue is stronger than the surrounding tissue that was not injured.

Every one of my scars has a story; everyone has a testimony of coming out on the other side.

Yet, we as men still cringe if someone touches our "boo-boo". We don't want anyone to touch the scar because we harbor the feelings of the wound, not the memory of the healing. In returning to my personal scars, they are a testimony to the mercy, patience and grace of God. Every one of my scars has a story; everyone has a testimony of coming out on the other side.

Up until this time, I have spoken of scars and scabs that can be seen. Yet, the vast majority of scars that a man possesses are not visible. They are emotional or psychological. It is here in the mind and heart that there needs to be a total disclosure of wounds concerning the healing power of God in a man's life. Once I discovered the power of testimony, I was elated! It didn't matter what was spoken over my life. It didn't matter the rejection, abuse and even neglect. All that mattered was that I could speak freely about it all; revealing the scars.

Regardless of what happened, there is a remedy for it in the Word of God.

There is a two-fold process to the confession aspect of our faith. The first process is to confess the pain, sin or shortcoming to God. It is here that we lose the battle because we think that God can't see the "thing" we are hiding. I make this the equivalent of playing kickball alone. You kick the ball of pain in the air and then catch it alone. You debate with yourself. "I'm out. No, I'm not". This is where the enemy tries to keep you; playing with your own logic. My son has coined a saying: kickboxing your own mind. Well, that would be the same as kicking yourself in your head and trying to knock your own self unconscious. It's ludicrous. We have to confess the pain in order for God to show us how to obtain the healing. The next aspect to confession is that we must confess the Word of God over that pain, agony and fear that comes about because of the wound. Regardless of what happened, there is a remedy for it in the Word of God. It is to our advantage to search the Scriptures learning what the remedy to our daily pain is. I say daily pain because there is not one day that we are alive where there is not some form of pain or reminder of past pain. Then the second part of the law of confession comes to the rescue. Confess His word over your world.

We have the testimony that is to be given freely not held as a hidden thing.

According to Deuteronomy 29:29, all secret things are God's possession, not ours. So, why are we trying to hold secrets? In Revelation 12:11 there is a two-fold process to overcome. We overcome by the Blood shed by Christ and also by the word of our testimony; talking about the scar. Too often we have the Blood requirement fully dealt with. However, we don't want to touch the testimony part. It's the testimony that we have an issue with.

The reputation is defended at all costs because we connect it with our worth and identity.

My brothers the enemy wants you to keep your testimony a secret which God said belongs to Him. We have the testimony that is to be given freely not held as a hidden thing. It is in the testimony that we cast off all garment of hiding our scars where others can freely see. I submit that it is not the testimony that we are concerned about, but our reputation! The reputation is defended at all costs because we connect it with our worth and identity. So, I ask why did Christ make Himself of "no reputation"? And, since this is true then why are we not following His example?

Christ invited people to touch His scars. And, with them touching His scars many came to believe on the Him as the Son of God rose from the dead. Could it be my brothers that we are hindering others from their life-changing encounters prohibiting them from displaying their scars to others? The bonfires of our scars are but the beacons of hope for others that are lost looking for refuge. It's time for us to allow those scars to be landmarks along the journey of deliverance and overcoming. Selah.

Reflection

Can you identify the source of your scars?

How can those scars identified be used as evangelistic tools?

Will you expose the scars in your life for His glory?

Do you think that Jesus exposed His scars?

Who We Were Created To Be

Man from the foundation of Creation has his purpose in God. He was made in the image of God and given authority over all the earth. This occurred before man was even placed on the earth in a physical body. He was in the spirit realm with God, not on earth at that juncture. However, we existed. We existed in the "image" and likeness of God; spirit. We were part of Him in essence, not apart from Him. We experienced His touch without hands or nerves. Yet, we experienced God in His fullness. This was our very first existence in a realm prior to being in a physical state.

> *"Then God said, "Let Us make man in Our image, according to Our likeness; let them have dominion over the fish of the sea, over the birds of the air, and over the cattle, over all the earth and over every creeping thing that creeps on the earth. So God created man in His own image; in the image of God He created him; male and female He created them. " Genesis 1:26, 27 KJV*

We should take note of the part where male and female are created together. God didn't create man then go back and create woman. We, men and women as one being, were existence emanating from God as a created being; waiting to be placed in the next phase of His purpose. We were not two separate entities in God's eyes. We were created as mankind, not man and woman, yet with a distinction of purpose as man and woman. I find much pleasure in reading the Jewish writings where the language paints a picture of things. It is robbery for the translations to omit certain expressions for the sake of cultural understanding. Perhaps this is why we have such a problem today in understanding the genders co-joining to form the complete man considered to be mankind. We were not given the truth about the woman being part of our existence. And, women were not given the revelation that we are essential to each other's destiny. Notice what the Apostle Paul says about men and women operating in one accord.

> *"Nevertheless, neither is man independent of woman, nor woman independent of man, in the Lord. For as woman came from man, even so man also comes through woman; **but all things are from God."** 1 Corinthians 11:11, 12 KJV*

The bold italics of the ending of the verse are my own to highlight that all things are from God. Now, since we were created in the spirit realm prior to being placed on earth, there seems to be a misconception of our position being one of dominance over a woman; or in today's society, even a woman dominating a man. The original "man" included both man and woman together. Alas, the passage that God gives us, "male and female, He created THEM" (Genesis 1:27 KJV). But, at this juncture we will concentrate on the male aspect of man.

Our original purpose was to worship and commune with Him.

We were made from the nothingness that only God could produce and begin using that same nothingness for a purpose. Notice what He says, "and the Lord God formed man of the dust of the ground and breathed into his nostrils the breath of life; and man became a living soul". (Genesis 2:7, KJV). This mighty God that we serve took nothing, made dust then made the body of man out of the dust. How awesome can that be within our limited understanding? Then He breathed His breath in us to make us a living soul. Apart from that we were still in the spirit realm and had no earthly license to represent God in this dimension. Now, once we became a living being in the earth realm, God began to give us a purpose. Our original purpose was to worship and commune with Him. This simple purpose has been distorted throughout time. Many ranging from theologians to the regular coffee break debaters have pushed their own agenda; often totally in error.

Part of our worship experience was derived from the work that God assigned us in the Garden and our total obedience to Him. In the spirit realm present with God we were in the presence of true worship! We were to tend the garden which was an extension of worship. Everything was in place for us to accomplish this worship act. We were to be the "source" on earth reflecting God in the heavenlies. Why? Jesus is the King of kings and the Lord of lords. By being made in His image, we require a kingdom to dominate or have dominion over. This kingdom is the earth, not heaven. Why would He create something to rule with Him in a place where only He could rule? But, yet He loved us enough to place us in our own custom made kingdom to begin operating in a manner consistent with His personality, being and character. We are made in His image and likeness, but not equal with Him. We are gods, but not the omniscient, omnipresent, and omnipotent God.

A person that is hurt and refuses healing speaks of the pain endured.

I can only use my own personal experiences and development for this work. Yes, I can use examples that may very well seem personal even possibly demeaning and damaging to some. But, I cannot give a person what I don't have. And, what I have is a personal deliverance and development that only the saving power of Jesus Christ provides. In this provision also comes the freedom and peace of being able to speak openly about it. "*And they overcame him by the blood of the Lamb, and by the word of their testimony; and they loved not their lives unto the death.*" (Revelation 12:10-12 KJV) Too often we will readily acknowledge the Blood of the Lamb, but restrict the word or our testimony which is the release of our deliverance and the connector of it to the universe and other people.

Fear is the first thing that contributes to all of our issues.

There is a deliverance that can only come with speech. Once you speak something, it is out there among us for the healing of many. A criminal confesses. He is free from the burden of secretive guilt although he may still embrace a measure of it. However, a son of God is free from the condemnation of guilt in Christ. A child cries. They have now called forth assistance and attention. A person that is hurt and refuses healing speaks of the pain endured. They can now begin to move through it unless they continually rehearse the pain. This is nothing new. God told us this in various places in the Word.

So what is it that our words can give such relief? It is the fact that we now have released it from within to be carried on the outside. Personally, as I released things, they were no longer festering within me as in times past. I held tightly to some things that were so painful that they began to foster hate, resentment, bitterness and revenge in me. We can allow things to perpetuate bitterness in us. Unforgiveness is the main thing that will burn in us. When we refuse to forgive, we are instructed firmly that we will not be forgiven. "But if ye forgive not men their trespasses, neither will your Father forgive your trespasses." (Matthew 6:15 KJV) A part of this unforgiveness comes when we don't speak what our shortcomings are. In essence when we come to Christ, we are acknowledging that we don't have the ability to be complete on our own. So, we freely acknowledge that apart from Christ we are incomplete and in need of a Savior. Often we are not allowing Him to be Lord at this time, but Savior.

As long as we carry the pain and anger, it will keep us in the prison of fear; tormenting fear.

The same is when we are injured and wounded as people; whether as children, youth or adults. It takes an acknowledgement and willingness to forgive for us to heal and continue to grow. What happens in unforgiveness is that we are placed in a prison of which we hold the key. This prison is not one that another places us in. It is a self-imposed prison that we choose to remain in until we forgive and also restricting our own forgiveness from the Father. As long as we carry the pain and anger, it will keep us in the prison of fear; tormenting fear. I remember someone telling me that anger is nothing but fear plus pain. As I reflected on that comment, I can see where all three of those aspects are needed to them to survive. They cannot survive in a damaging state alone. They must be coexistent. It is like the three dimensions of God. The Father, Son and Holy Spirit are One. This is the reciprocal of dysfunction; fear, anger and pain.

Fear is the first thing that contributes to all of our issues. Fear of missing out. Fear of not having something which is in direct conflict with God's word and promises. Fear of not making the mark; again in conflict to our existence in

God. This fear begins as a thought and escalates to a spirit. And, death is the foundation of all fear. It was the fear of death or separation from God that prevented Adam and Eve from partaking of the fruit. God told Adam that if he ate of the fruit he would surely die. Even though death was not anything he had experienced, he feared it. Once the righteous fear of death was deceitfully removed, the enemy could replace it with an *unrighteous* yet real fear of death instituting a spirit of fear. The resurrection of our Lord and Savior Jesus destroyed the sting and fear of death. So, we have no fear of it now. God tells us firmly:

> *"God has not given us the spirit of fear, but of power, of love and of a sound mind." (2 Timothy 1:7 KJV)*

Lust is a byproduct of fear. I say this because of the first conversation with the enemy in the Garden of Eden. I would be hard pressed to believe that there was no sense of bliss and satisfaction with Adam and Eve. Even though the Bible had not yet been recorded as of yet, all of God's promises were already in effect. We know that in His presence is fullness of joy. We know that He supplies all of our needs according to His riches in glory. Yet, in all of this, mankind chose to be fearful that they were missing out on something. This caused much pain for everyone involved, especially us. God had already laid out the plan of life for them. He even told them which tree they could not eat of and why. But, the fear of Someone keeping something from them was too much for mankind to bear when the deceiver twisted the instructions given them. They allowed someone to make them question the validity and sincerity of God. This began a perpetual cycle that can only be broken with the Blood of Jesus.

We were told that we could not eat of the Tree of the Knowledge of Good and Evil. I submit that we could! Before you rush back to receive a refund for this writing please travel with me on a journey in the Book of Genesis. In Genesis 2:9 the record indicates that God caused every tree to grow from the ground. The Tree of Life and the Tree of the Knowledge of Good and Evil were both there and no restriction to the access to them. As a matter of fact in Genesis 2:15-18 the record states that God placed the man in the Garden to dress and keep it with the "instruction", not restriction that IF he ate of the fruit he would surely die (separation from God). I could not find any original text, translation or anything that said that Adam was not to touch the tree! How can you dress and keep something yet do not touch it? And, with the coming of Eve, she was to be a help meet. Therefore, she was to be able to touch it too.

God told him to not eat of the tree even though he could touch it.

Yet, in the dressing and keeping of the Garden including both trees, they were not to eat of any tree or herb that did not have seed. I submit to you that the

Tree of the Knowledge of Good and Evil needed a means of reproduction since it had no "seed". It was a hybrid of sorts; good and evil. Man became that "seed" to perpetuate that mixed knowledge or worldly wisdom into the earth. Again, man was never told not to touch the trees. But, God allowed him free will, not freedom of choice. God told him to not eat of the tree even though he could touch it. In another way to give this, you can lick a hot pot in our own ability. That doesn't make it a great and wonderful idea. Adam could eat of this tree apart from what God directed and command him, but as we see it wasn't such a wise idea.

Pain on the other hand is also a cohort of fear and anger. One definition of pain is "mental or emotional suffering". We all have the physical understanding of pain. But, the mental and emotional suffering can be even more devastating and deadly. It can cause self-destructive behaviors, social and emotional distancing, religious abuses and even physical maladies. Again, as I stated previously I would only use my personal examples thereby not ever breaching the confidentiality of any other person. My own experiences are my own. They are lodged in my mind and often hidden deep within subconscious chasms of protective non-recollections. Yet, they do surface and must be dealt with. Triggers cause them to rise to consciousness and receive the attention needed for deliverance. The first order of attention will always be forgiveness; the offender, then yourself. There will never be deliverance without forgiveness.

My suffering, mental, emotional and physical, began as a youth at home. However, the mindset leading my own treatment did not begin with me. It was a generational and familial curse and spirit reaching back beyond the present person. Much like many other perpetual errors and doctrines, it began with one person and was passed down without ever being challenged on both sides of my lineage. As Dr. Hart Ramsey, pastor of the Northview Christian Church in Dothan, Alabama stated so eloquently, "God needed the function of your parents to be in you. Unfortunately, you also inherited their dysfunction as well." This proved so very true in my own life and existence. While I may not go into gross and intimate details I will say that both parents were abusive in my life. Siblings were abusive. Family members were abusive. Therefore, I had much to seek healing from. Again, forgiveness is the key in all things; especially your own healing and deliverance. Heal the boy, help the man. Help the man, heal the house. Heal the house. Create a healthy community which in turn will create a healthy land.

As a veteran, I often wondered how many military people request hazardous duty or special training to boost self-esteem.

Now in a challenging thought, there are many men in society that originated from maladies similar if not the same as mine. However, the society that attempts to dictate them being a man also dictates that they never reveal the emotions and effects of rejection, abuse, abandonment and low self-esteem. As a veteran, I often wondered how many military people request hazardous duty or special training to boost self-esteem. I was one of them. And, even prior to that, I was known on the streets to take risks that others wouldn't take to build up my own self-esteem and acceptance. I know that inside my house was madness and pain.

A controlling personality and spirit is one birthed out of fear.

Therefore, outside my front door I was controlling my destiny to the best of my ability so I thought. That was nothing but fear of being hurt. And, in that fear, I hurt many people who may have had the same fear that I did. A controlling personality and spirit is one birthed out of fear. You must go back and find that "thing" or "person" that injured you and address it. Forgive those involved. Forgive yourself if you did partake of something you knew better. Release the pain and embrace the love of God to fill that void; agape, unconditional love.

We speak things into existence just like God does.

In essence, who we were created to be and who we became by choice are in direct conflict with one another. God created us in His image and likeness. Yet, we through our own disobedience decided to do something different and do our own thing which caused death. Yet, the original intent of God stands firm in us being created in His image and likeness and to worship Him. We speak things into existence just like God does. We create things from our minds just like He does. God gives us a thought or invention and we create it from the thought in our mind. Man commands the environment, just like God does. Often we don't command it wisely, be we do command it. One may debate it, because of the scale of command, but take for instance irrigation. The environment is commanded to displace water and relocate the flow to another avenue. We have commanded the environment to do so. And, we love unconditionally just like He does. Again, there may be disagreement. But, we love like He does because it is a decision. So, if we do not, we have made the decision not to. When we pick and choose which attributes and to whom we decide to love, then we err totally from His presence and purpose.

Reflection

Exactly who were you created to be?

Can you express your pain at a point in life without reliving it?

Since our identity is in God, how do we express it to others?

So What Happened?

Often our childhood influences our concept of manhood and even fatherhood so powerfully that we carry this influence throughout life. Media has done such a disservice to the development of children until we must be ever-wary of releasing our supervision of our children over to media or even education and schools. Images of an uncaring and aloof father flood the media with such intensity that one has to wonder who actually wrote these sitcoms and what their fathers were like. Other aspects of fatherhood in the media portray fathers as individuals who are either henpecked, escapists of reality or those who live for yesterday instead of directing the family in a progressive direction. Then of course there are the weekend warriors with the boys who engage in so much debauchery until one cannot tell the adolescent from the man except for the beard and balding cranium.

Childhood, while to be a memorable and happy time, can often be filled with stress and trouble given the freedom that we now have in society. This period of life is also to be a developmental period for the individual who was born on this earth. God's word is so full of direction for raising children. Sadly, too often parents don't turn to His instruction in raising and preparing their children. Instead we turn to the gurus of media and psychology for guidance with their secular and often damaging formulas for parenting. Even our ancestral examples can be utterly destructive in raising a child; causing emotional, psychological and even other damage to the child influencing the rest of the child's adult life.

I don't think it is just social values, but a lack of spiritual values will definitely take society to a new low.

I often wonder what guidance was given to those who parented offspring convicted of heinous crimes or even those who committed very violent crimes or whether they received any at all. Were the parents knowledgeable and led by the Word of God in their parenting, or did they perpetuate the mistakes and myths of their ancestors? There is a misconception that certain social values make a case for crime. I don't think it is just social values, but a lack of spiritual values will definitely take society to a new low. Take God out of the picture and you have total chaos: guaranteed. Yes, there are those who raise seemingly productive children. However, in the absence of observing populations, what struggles and questions do they pose without the original purpose of God? As the spirit man is starved and restricted, the manifestation will truly be reflected in the natural.

Reflection

What do you see that has happened?

What images of a father has media presented to you that were humorous but not appalling?

Were you raised with a Biblical view?

Fathers

Think back to your own childhood. What was your perception of manhood? Was it functional? Did it serve you well in your growth toward Christ and godliness? Was God even the central figure in our instruction? The initial influence for fatherhood was given to us by an earthly father, or father-figure. If there was no masculine figure then our initial observation was from another source that was not the intended representative and does reflect in the life of the male child. Not only does this influence what we think manhood is, but also it influences how we view our Heavenly Father and how He is to react to us.

Being the product of Depression era parents, their views continually surfaced in my own life as a truth and norm for them.

A point to be pondered is that of a child who views the father figure as authoritarian. Once that person comes to Christ and is to view our Heavenly Father through his own experiences, it will be difficult at best to relate to a caring and merciful father. If the child has only viewed "Daddy" as one who would fly off the handle at any given moment, there will be only the terrifying fear of God that will strike him dead if a mistake is made.

In my own life, I am sure that my perception of father was shaped not by my father, but by his ancestors. No one can give you what they never had unless they find a source to supply their need. Being the product of Depression era parents, their views continually surfaced in my own life as a truth and norm for them.

A personal example comes to mind. For whatever reasons, I don't possess many old photographs of my youthful and younger years. Whether they were pilfered, lost or just didn't exist, these times are not documented as much as latter times. But, recently after looking through some old photographs in which I discovered one of a very fond Christmas. I was just as happy as could be with a present that I received. In the background sat my grandfather. He was very aloof to me for the time that I knew him; borderline not even wanting me in his presence. He sat in his favorite chair by the window looking out. I had invaded his space with my Play-Dough and was enjoying most likely the only true toy gift that year. But, at this particular junction in my life I viewed everything else around in this photo. Everything was of poverty even though I knew there was some form of income coming in the home! Discarded books, used furniture, and I even had on hand-me-downs, for Christmas! While I still do herald that as the most memorable Christmas that I had, I also understand now that the spirit of poverty and dysfunction began well before my existence and had to be broken.

The foundational truths of the father-son relationship and instruct all point to the relationship between God the Father and God the Son.

However, in coming into a saving and liberating knowledge of Christ, I am able to process every thought, perception and memory through the Word of God for a healthy example of manhood. And, it is better late than never. I never gave up desiring to know the truth and searching out examples. Yes, there are Biblical figures that would dispute to the selective reader the example of fatherhood. However, we are always directed back in the teachings of Christ to our Heavenly Father and His attributes. The foundational truths of the father-son relationship and instruct all point to the relationship between God the Father and God the Son. A foundation can be laid yet the structure can be altered. In no way does it destroy the integrity of the foundation.

I had to become one with the One that birthed the church.

Fathers are a peculiar group. As men, many are not necessarily the most affectionate and nurturing. This is why the mother plays a vital role in fatherhood as well. What we have not been endowed totally with (for we do have a measure of nurturing), the mother compliments us. As we are transparent and begin to learn and observe, we, too can become very nurturing without threatening our manhood and actually enjoy it. As a child, to my memory, I never received any affection or nurturing from my father. He never received any from his father from our discussions later in his life. Does that resolve me of any responsibility to actively seek correction in this area? No. However, I must draw on the things that were positive about my youth, incorporate them into the present and equip my children for the future as best I can. And, the best equipping of my children occurred the day that I received Jesus Christ as my personal Savior and made Him Lord over my life to teach me all things! It was not just enough to "join the church". I had to become one with the One that birthed the church. Just because one does not know all of the facets of fatherhood will in no way release him to perpetuate ignorance. Again, we have an example to strive toward; God the FATHER.

Why give someone power over your life?

If one is not careful, he will mirror his father in all aspects; positive and negative. The same concept is used as an abuser of sorts. If one has been abused as a child in any manner, often they grow up to be abusers in some manner. If one has witnessed certain destructive behaviors as a child, they will most likely mirror those behaviors as men and sadly fathers. I witnessed many detestable and destructive behaviors as a child; both by father and mother. The pattern had to be broken. However, since coming to Christ, I yearned to be who He said I am. Sadly enough, these desires can cause family rifts and shine a light on those things that people don't want illuminated because there are times when accounts have to be given. I am in no way promoting that a person air family dirty laundry where it needs to be covered in love. While yes, there must be some form of facing the fact, event or speech. After that comes forgiveness in order for you to grow and be at peace, not the offender. And, I would even challenge a person as to whether the speaking of a thing publically would benefit existence other than to make one feel guilty. Even in that vein there are times when the perpetrator will not feel any remorse and even attempt to make the victim seem as the transgressor. So, it is my prayer that one would seek the Lord's wisdom on such issues.

Why give someone power over your life? There are things that very few people knew. And, they only knew because I entrusted such pain to them in order for my healing to occur. Now, had I continued repeating and telling everyone, there would no doubt be much more family turmoil. I would listen to my mother in her elderly years speaking of how she knew certain things of my father and how she would take it to her grave. At the same time, other family members were telling me things concerning him. Yet, I knew things concerning both parents and some siblings. With all of this said, I made an informed decision to allow love to cover it with the decision of forgiveness and the determination to love with joy. And, while at times some thoughts may attempt to sneak back, I can remind (re: make new, mind: my thoughts) that I have chosen to forgive them as God forgave me. Were they traumatic? YES! Were they painful? YES! Did they cause harm? For many years, YES! Am I at peace in forgiveness? Definitely yes!!!

We are fathers not to rule by fear, but by compassion and wisdom.

A man must understand that telling events and pains can justify in many ways why you act a way or do certain things. But, it will boil down to whether you wish to be right, or would you rather be righteous? And, all righteousness is of God who said He would not remember (never forget for it is an involuntary action) our sins anymore. Again, re means to do again, and member means to construct a thing. So, since I am made in His image, I need to do a lot less remembering and much more creating.

A breakthrough for me was when I spoke with my youngest son concerning an issue. I wanted to know what he was thinking. I needed to know where his little mind was. In response and full of fear he stated that he "feared" me. This was strong yet honest language for a child to portray to his father. However, at that very moment, I realized that I was mirroring my father's actions and the desired results; control by tyranny. We are fathers not to rule by fear, but by compassion and wisdom. Colossians 3:21 KJV states, "*Fathers, do not provoke your children, let they become discouraged.*" My son was discouraged and full of fear. As I poured through my past, my father often did the same to me. I even witnessed his father doing it to him as a grown man and my grandfather was well progressed in age. That point of healing and breakthrough was very painful, but needed.

Correction is not about abuse or control. It's about love.

This day, I have a very open relationship with my son for the most part. He is able to speak to me concerning everything. We can communicate on another level. However, I am still his father. I am his best friend, but he is not mine. And, there was a time when I had to "warm him up" when he thought he was my equal. There must be healthy boundaries set in the parental relationship; both paternal and maternal. What is the reward? I see him in his interaction with his son. While I do not meddle in parental affairs only offering advice and reminding him of his upbringing, I do offer some guidance that may save him many later corrections and also pain to the little one. I find it somewhat comical how my son will "warm up" my grandson at the drop of a hat if something perverse comes out of his mouth. When I ask him why, he simply tells me, "So he won't act up like I did." I almost had tears of laughter in my eyes one time in witnessing this. But, he has the idea. Correction is not about abuse or control. It's about love.

At his death he was discovered to be a well-educated and financially well-to-do man.

One may ask where they can find a father figure if there was not one present. Well, it may not be as hard as you think. Again, begin with God the Heavenly Father which is the epitome of Fatherhood. He will truly guide and direct you to an earthly reference. There are those in society that may not be biological fathers, but surrogate or spiritual fathers. An example that I can truly remember is speaking to one of the neighborhood alcoholics. Regardless of what I didn't get at home, he did give me some of the wisdom that was needed.

While laced with some vulgarities, we understood the message he was delivering.

His name was Jimmy. At his death he was discovered to be a well-educated and financially well-to-do man. Yet, for whatever reasons he chose to walk the streets as an alcoholic and even clandestinely helping others financially. They had no idea until he died. In one particular time a neighborhood friend and I had a crush on the same girl; a new girl. He saw me get a kiss one day. It was not good for our friendship to say the least. We arrived at the place of combat in the alley behind the cleaners in the empty lot. That's where all the disputes of the neighborhood were settled apart from the prying eyes of parents that would call your parents. The neighborhood hoards showed up. Then we disturbed Jimmy who was taking a nap under the tree with a grip on his bottle of Wild Irish Rose. Not a good thing to do. He got both of us and gave us a quick talking to concerning juvenile love. While laced with some vulgarities, we understood the message he was delivering. We never fought that day and left the alley better friends and reserved that neither of us would pursue this girl. She was trouble and proved it later.

We spent a lot of time listening to Jimmy after that because he offered us some wisdom. While I had a father at home who was present but absent, my friend didn't. He was a foster child and only knew the parents and other foster siblings that were in the house where he was now living. So, we could supplement our needs with Jimmy which was invaluable in many ways.

I experienced more distress and grief over his passing away than I did with my own biological father.

There are many examples of fatherly wisdom being given to me. Another example would be my stepfather. After my father passed away, my mother married a wonderful man who actually knew us as children. One of my father's friends in life had lost his wife only months after my father passed. In the years to come, he and my mother became closer friends and suddenly married. That man, I affectionately called him Mr. Mac, provided much of the guidance that I needed for a paradigm shift in fatherhood. He was very instrumental in me looking honestly at the dysfunction in my thought process and seeking to improve for the sake of my walk with God. He was nothing like my father at all! I wondered how they were ever friends! This man was educated, loved to read and patient as the day was long; especially with my younger brother who tried to give him a fit at first. I experienced more distress and grief over his passing away than I did with my own biological father. Yet, I still to this day give honor to my father. I didn't say I like what he did and things he caused. But, I give honor because of the Word of God which also tells me to love (agape) everyone but not necessarily like them.

While men don't speak of things for fear of being labeled less manly, often it is the pain of hurting others that may cause the silence.

Certainly I cannot ignore another figure who was a cross between an elder brother and father; Richard McNeil. Although he was my brother-in-law, he would give such advice and guidance as to bring Godly wisdom to earth. I treasured the many times we had conversations about life. In him I did confide many things that I trusted would not leak in the atmosphere; things that would damage the perceived image of our family and members that were no longer among us. Yet, there were things that I withheld from him as well. His first loyalty concerning confidentiality was to my sister; his wife. Brothers, this is a lesson to be taught. The two becoming one involves both parts of the two having the same knowledge. Now, at his transition, I decided to continue to hold onto those things that while painful have no purpose in righteousness or edification. Perhaps if some would embrace true healing and choose to understand that because many don't speak doesn't mean they would not have something to say, then hoards could heal. While men don't speak of things for fear of being labeled less manly, often it is the pain of hurting others that may cause the silence. Such was the case with me. For decades I have never spoken a word of certain things that would devastate the image of certain others. It's not my place. God had given me the grace to hold such things between Him and me.

One conversation that we shared was concerning being right versus righteous. It was one of our last conversations telephonically in June of 2007. In that conversation, which by the way was concerning childhood trauma that I witnessed and later endured, I remember him asking me why I was concerned with being righteous and what was the difference in being right. It was only the Holy Spirit guiding me in the answer that I gave. I told him that in order to be right I had to continually prove someone else to be wrong in order to stay right; constantly holding them down and having "something over them". But, in order for me to be righteous, I only had to trust God in what was done was already forgiven first by me, then by Him if the person asked for it. Either way, my righteousness had to be in God and not me. My righteousness is described as filthy rags according to the Word of God. And, while God doesn't continually accuse me, I won't continually accuse and relive the events.

This is the test of a father; the ability to teach as he walks.

Our conversation went on for close to an hour. The last thing that he said was that he understood that my (meaning my own) righteousness didn't involve others. Yet he still didn't understand how I could do it so easily. I told him, that the ease didn't come from me. It came from God. His next statement blew me away. He said that since God had to give peace with such (explicative) things then that's the only way to get peace. Then I knew he understood me. We didn't have many conversations after that. But, every conversation he shared with me had a lesson in it; even those shared in humor and stupor. This is the test of a father; the ability to teach as he walks.

Finally, there are spiritual fathers who birth sons and daughters in accordance with God's word. Malachi 2:15 speaks of God desiring godly seed from us. Understanding that the man is the keeper of the seed, we are to provide His seed, through us to produce this. This aspect of fatherhood is much more stringent that just being a biological or social father. It has implications that are far reaching and also will be answered for directly to the Father. Alas, fatherhood in any format or dimension is not to be taken lightly.

Let me please make clear the seed concept of man. As stated earlier, mankind consists of two genders; male and female. There is a concept that neither can operate without the other. Male needs female. And, female needs male. This concept recorded in I Corinthians 11:11-12 KJV is:

> *Nevertheless, neither is man independent of woman, nor woman independent of man, in the Lord. For as woman came from man, even so man also comes through woman; but all things are from God.*

There is no way that one can say state the male gender is all encompassing without the female gender. God the Father is the original Source with us, the human reproducing after our own kind. Prior to the fall, we would have produced after the fully functional and joyful Adam and Eve. After the fall, our source became Adam apart from God. Before the fall our source would have been the perfect Adam with God. Now, in Christ, our Source is Jesus in God; Perfection at its best!

Reflection

Who did you give power over your life?

Has the connection to father been resolved?

What advice would you give a young man who didn't have a father figure?

True Riches of a Man

Man is also to possess riches in order to function properly in the earth; especially in the Kingdom of God. His riches according to society and historically been those of monetary value. While this is truly a tangible evidence of riches, there are other facets that have more intrinsic value. There are riches that excel any value that fiduciary success can give you. These riches are hidden in plain view in the Bible. While there may be many people suggesting that some interpretation of the Bible is not to be even considered, I beg to differ. Those that can hear the voice of God in certain presentations and spiritually understand the message need to shed imbedded theology in order to receive the message. Such is the message of the true riches of man. It must be understood first in the spirit man before even coming to the soulish man. It is a spiritual message to be received in the spirit man first.

In Luke 16 we see the record of the unjust steward parable. While in numerous times I have heard messages on honesty, thriftiness and even discovery of your deeds being lifted from there. Yet, in prayer I heard to look at a different illumination; riches. I was perplexed as I began the task of learning the measurements of the particular payment methods, amounts and substances. And, I was getting nowhere. Finally, I just got quiet before the Lord and heard what He was saying to me. It took humility to look at how some training and education actually gave me the tool to see something that many do not understand. The "law of first mention" of systematic theology instructed me to look at a thing when it was first mentioned in the Bible before we allow it to be used. This way there will be no mistake in what is being described. In other words, I cannot look at the fall in the Garden and then say that a message on growing tomatoes can be presented to God's people. So this is what I did with what God was speaking.

Luke 16:1-13 records this parable:
> *And he said also unto his disciples, There was a certain rich man, which had a steward; and the same was accused unto him that he had wasted his goods. And he called him, and said unto him, How is it that I hear this of thee? give an account of thy stewardship; for thou mayest be no longer steward. Then the steward said within himself, What shall I do? for my lord taketh away from me the stewardship: I cannot dig; to beg I am ashamed. I am resolved what to do, that, when I am put out of the stewardship, they may receive me into their houses. So he called every one of his lord's debtors unto him, and said unto the first, How much owest thou unto my lord? And he said, An hundred measures of oil. And he said unto him, Take thy bill, and sit down quickly, and write fifty. Then said he to another, And how much owest thou? And he said, An hundred measures of wheat. And he said unto him, Take thy bill, and write fourscore. And the lord commended the unjust steward, because he had done wisely: for the children of this world are in their generation*

wiser than the children of light. And I say unto you, Make to yourselves friends of the mammon of unrighteousness; that, when ye fail, they may receive you into everlasting habitations. He that is faithful in that which is least is faithful also in much: and he that is unjust in the least is unjust also in much. If therefore ye have not been faithful in the unrighteous mammon, who will commit to your trust the true riches? And if ye have not been faithful in that which is another man's, who shall give you that which is your own? No servant can serve two masters: for either he will hate the one, and love the other; or else he will hold to the one, and despise the other. Ye cannot serve God and mammon.

In the beginning of the parable we observe an unjust steward being discovered by his master or manager for embezzling funds. The master actually tells the unjust steward that he will be fired after he gives an account of all the outstanding debts. In this fear, the steward imagines all scenarios. He can't beg when he's fired. No doubt others will ridicule him. He's been too pampered to dig ditches. His only possibility for an escape and survival depended on the relationships he had formed over time with the master's debtors. This way if the dreadful day came, there would be someone to take him into their home until he again is employed.

These people had "paid in full" documents from the head of the collections department that could not be challenged!

Immediately he calls them to him because they do not yet know he is to be fired. He instructed one to pay fifty measures of the one hundred measures of oil he owed. The next, he instructed the debtor to pay eighty measures of the one hundred measures of wheat that he owed. In other words, there was a relationship formed previously that was being strengthened even in this trying time. These people had "paid in full" documents from the head of the collections department that could not be challenged! Imagine the joy they had knowing that not only had the debt been resolved, but the debt was resolved for much less than the original debt. To insure that there can be no stretching of this, it was commanded in Leviticus 25:35-38 that no usury (interest) could be charged. So, in essence one man received a fifty percent deduction in the original debt while another received a twenty percent deduction. Either way, the relationships were strengthened. This man had a place to live because of the relationships that were formed and strengthened.

The master commended the unjust steward in the account.

So, what is the connection between these business deals, even though less than ethical and the riches I speak of? In the Book of Genesis God speaks of something that we take for granted; relationship. In order for Him to speak as a collective Trinity, there has to be relationship. This is where the first mention of a true relationship between like Beings begins. When God spoke

47

"let Us", He in essence identified the very first relationship ever; Himself in the Persons of the Father, Son and Holy Spirit. These are the true riches that we are to possess. This man forged such relationships until he ensured he would have a place to stay, clothes on his back and food to eat while he began to regroup and move on. Never did the account state that he was absolved of his wrongdoing. It was still past event. He was wrong for whatever reasons. But, his future looked a lot better because of his present relationships! As a matter of fact, his true riches of relationships also touched the relationship of his master. The master commended the unjust steward in the account. Again, we always warn people not to read anything into the Biblical accounts. This time I issue a warning to not read anything out of it. The termination of the unjust steward was never finalized. The parable ends with the unjust steward being praised by his master, not fired.

... I never saw where God told someone that they couldn't serve Him and the enemy.

In the end Jesus issued a stern instruction which tells us that riches are not monetary. Jesus states in Luke 16:13 that man cannot serve God and mammon. This seems very odd if you were looking at this parable as a business lesson. But, in my reading of the Bible, I never saw where God told someone that they couldn't serve Him and the enemy. Yet, in the King James Version of the Bible money as a word is mentioned numerous. This does not include the times that finances are mentioned in the form of lands, livestock, houses and servants. So, for Jesus to make this declaration there must be two things in this parable that are paramount to riches. First, riches have no fiduciary value yet are priceless. And, finally, if you serve the money instead of letting the money serve God through you, the primary relationship with God is non-existent. Now, we have a man's true riches. His true riches begin with God and extend to our neighbors. Selah.

Reflection

What are your true riches?

Can you help someone else become free by writing off your charges?

Since I have never heard Jesus say that He is disappointed in someone, will you follow suit?

Our Instructions

Genesis records the creation of all the earth and everything alive in it. In essence, it is the blueprint for all that is on the earth, including man. In my own Bible, I have put much wear and tear on the first four chapters of Genesis. Why? Whenever I have a question as to God's intention for me in the earth, I go back to when He walked with Adam and how they interacted. It may not implicitly state that "God talked with Adam and therefore Adam wanted to taste strawberries". But, the account does imply that God and Adam shared intimacy. In order to be closely intimate sometimes the loudest conversations you may have will be silence. The most fulfilling times in the presence of God has been with our silence but overwhelmed by just His presence.

Apostle Nate Holcomb, a mighty man of God, says that the church at its birth is the church at its best. There is no argument to this. For even in the waiting period before being baptized in the Holy Spirit, there was the intimacy of prayer. Then when the Holy Spirit fell upon them, there was nothing said until the disciples present began speaking in other tongues. So, in both Testaments, I can see where worship and presence is much more important and rewarding that work and human preparation. While I do not negate any part of working or preparation, I will not give it the preeminence over His presence and worship. It is in His presence that I can know His mind while seeing what He sees. And, that will ensure that I will be as Christ; only doing what I see Him do and saying what I hear Him saying. It is here where our relationship is born, strengthened and solidified.

> ### *The most fulfilling times in the presence of God has been with our silence but overwhelmed by just His presence.*

It is in His presence where I don't have to concern myself with anything but Him. We get our instructions by listening to His silent presence which fills us with all knowledge and understanding. Adam was in His presence just walking with Him. What happened? He received every name of every creature on the earth. He reached a point of intimacy that overflowed to Eve upon her arrival. He knew nothing but the cool of the day and being cool every day. Then when it was time to know Eve, he even received instructions concerning that! It was like needing to know something but not needing to learn what you needed.

It's in the Presence that we learn everything that is needed. Sadly, we as men have received instructions from everywhere but His presence. We find instructions on everything from the internet, our friends, relatives and even church. But, we have turned away from the instructions received just by being in His presence. It is truly time for us to return to His presence and just sit! While it may not be a physical place to return to, it is a spiritual place that can be reached even on a crowded street or in a large church congregation.

I recently heard a sermon where we are to be carriers of His presence. This is what Adam was. He was a carrier of the presence of God! Wherever he went, the presence of God was with Him. Why? There was a residual presence and fragrance upon him when he left the presence of God. Adam preceded Jesus in carrying God's presence. So, here we come; those who are in Christ. Now, we are the carriers of His presence.

I began to pay particular attention to the life Jesus lived in reference to prayer, miracles and just time spent in the presence of God. It is recorded that He was up well before the rest of the disciples. He went into a private place; the mountains. The disciples saw this yet didn't join Him. When Jesus returned, He was ready for the day of ministry. Could it be that our time in ministry whether to family or others is so draining because of the lack of prayer intimacy? And, prayer is not always asking. It is more listening and worshipping than asking for something! The unspoken language of total joy overcomes me when I am "there" in His presence. I don't have to say anything. Adam didn't have to say anything. He just "was".

I just want "Him" which is everything I ever desired whether out of want or need.

My tears are mixed. They are tears of total joy in His presence. And, they are also tears of sadness that I never experienced this prior to this season of my life. When I speak of it to others there can be attacks or ridicule. The Presence that I experience is on me regardless of where I am. I can be in the middle of the most hideous place on this planet. Yet, I am still in His presence. Can this be considered crazy? Most definitely! It makes no logical sense but all spiritual sense! Hell can be breaking lose all around me. Yet, here I am in such a worshipful state until I just weep! I don't want anything from Him. I just want "Him" which is everything I ever desired whether out of want or need.

This is the instruction we are given hidden in plain view. It's in Him that we live, move and have our being! Get into Him. Follow the instruction of the Word of God made flesh and the Word of God recorded on paper. Get into Him and stay there. This way you will never operate on your own misconception of power and anointing. You will always be in Him. And, in Him there can be nothing but love. Our instructions are simple. Seek Him. Find Him. Abide in Him. Worship Him. Become carriers of His Presence. And, finally we are to permeate the earth with Him! Selah!

Reflection

How many times do you stay present in His presence?

Do you wait for instructions or "just do it"?

Do you understand the instructions given by the Holy Spirit?

The Blood of the Lamb and the Word of Our Testimony

We as men understand the blood atonement of the Lamb of God slain before the foundation of the earth. However, the word of our testimony may cast a perceived negative light on our existence which is not in keeping with our desired image. It may often involve fear, rejection, molestation, anger, and a host of other maladies that would attack our image in our own mind and the minds of others. Yet, we have no clue that these are the very chains keeping us in bondage to the enemy! It is the trick of the enemy to have all not confess or expose these things in our past which will keep us in a condemned state when God said that we are not under condemnation once we come to Christ.

A friend of mine, Hans Nelson, spoke something that I found awesomely simplistic. Yet, I could see where he may have a problem if he spoke this same truth in highly religious settings where the works of the Law is at work over the gift of grace in Christ. He said, "Anything that I may fall in is not mine to possess because Christ already took it to the Cross. Yet, anything that I do good concerning is not mine to boast of either because it is only God using me to do His will". I was floored at the simplicity of his statement. I attempted to share it with someone and was overheard by a highly religious person. I guess the Christian regalia around his neck, on his clothes and bags gave him away. He immediately came to me and tried to argue the point that we must work to earn our way.

Anything that I may fall in is not mine to possess because Christ already took it to the Cross.

Allow me to give a word of wisdom to all disciples. We are not to argue the Word of God with anyone. Never give place to argue. Bless the person in your presence and leave. And, this is just what we did. But, as we walked that rhema marinated again causing a spontaneous praise! It is moments like this when we must be vigilant with an open ear to the Master's voice. So, when this concept is mastered, our testimony can flow. At first, it may be selective in audience and in detail. But, as we understand the truth that God has taken this all of this to the Cross and atoned for it all, we are free not to brag on what used to be, but to show how everyone can be free through the power of Christ.

I found myself not wanting to tell anyone at all what I had gone through even though much of it was well hidden in the history of youthfulness. At that time I couldn't speak to my family members that I trusted out of shame and even anger. And it was family the caused the pain; well revered members of the family. I could not confront the persons involved because of familial positions and the anger that I had toward them. Yet, I found myself defending them at all costs ever remembering the pain inflicted. Finally, I confronted and laid it all out to my mother of what happened, when it happened and who was responsible including her. I spoke very candidly, yet sympathetically on how it made me feel and shaped my life and behaviors. She initially rejected everything said and became quite hostile; constantly voicing poison concerning me, my life and appearance. I in turn spent quite a few years attempting to please her in any way possible thinking that I was at fault in many of the terrors. Surely, it must have been me because no one else would have had this inflicted. Then I came to my senses. It wasn't me. Nor was it the other family members involved in things that occurred. And, if it was initiated or allowed by turning a blind eye, then there was fault in that action as well. I spoke, held my ground and moved on to forgiveness with a quickness that I could heal and begin life as it was intended. It was not an overnight thing. Yet, it was an immediate forgiveness regardless of what I felt, knowing that I would have to discipline myself to remain forgiving and not reliving or repeating it. I need for the reader to understand beyond a shadow of a doubt that forgiveness is more for you than anyone else! Surely the transgressor needs your forgiveness. But, you stand to gain more by quickly forgiving. If we don't forgive, then God cannot forgive us. And, this must not be lip service. It must be in action and complete.

We are free not to brag on what used to be, but to show how everyone can be free.

Years later in life my mother and I had a very long conversation in which I assured her that I had forgiven her for all in the past when I said I did, and I had forgiven all involved. No, I didn't forget it. But, I had forgiven her and would not "re" "member" it. To her or anyone I had forgiven, I would not put it back together in her presence again because of the completeness of forgiveness. It was a God-ordained teaching moment in which I discovered she had not forgiven many people in her own life. It was at that moment that the healing power of forgiveness was discovered and embraced.

I will tell anyone that constantly "remembers" things; you are still in bondage and full of bitterness that spills over in many different areas of your life; all fueled by murder and pride. While you may think you have joy, it is not full as God intended. I would even venture to say that any confession that you have is a mechanical and rote recitation concerning God with no real desire for intimacy. Why? Because, when you have unforgiveness it makes it impossible to experience joy and peace. I could not experience intimacy with God until I allowed Him to show me where I was harboring bitterness and constantly replaying painful events in my psyche. While I thought I was free, I only had transparent chains that were still holding me; tighter than any visible shackles could. As a matter of fact some of our chains have been decorated as to be used as jewelry or badges of reasoning for our current hate and behavior.

It was at that moment that the healing power of forgiveness was discovered and embraced.

I began to destroy my chains of bitterness and unforgiveness once it all came crashing down on me at the passing of my stepfather. I had begun speaking to him on a more intimate level concerning the past and present things for manhood. Between him and my brother-in-law, Richie, I gleaned ways of functioning with the pain which were effective, but not healing. Yet, I wanted more as to not be in pain and producing but being pain free. As I began getting closer to "Mr. Mack" I began discovering that he was a godsend in providing me wise ways to deal with the issues at hand. I discovered long after his transition that my mother had no idea that I would talk to him as often. The wise and instructional conversations we shared were kept between us. This really gave me a sense of awe concerning him. I recall him saying, "Some people will never admit or apologize for the pain they caused you. So, you have to be willing to forgive even if they deny it ever happened". This was the case with family members. Only one after a few years did apologize and ask for forgiveness out of the blue. But, I had already forgiven. So, to ease their mind and soul, I accepted and told them that they had been forgiven a long time before that moment. They were ready to transition into God's presence. I guess this was something that was needed for their soul prior to the transition.

In cases of such injustice, there are two ways you deal with it. The first and often the most widely used techniques are to defend, serve and seek approval concerning the one that has injured you; even at an unhealthy level. The next way results in total hatred that bitterly eats away at you as a cancer that you wish to spread by telling others often with the intent and desire to murder that person with your words. While it may be considered a warning of dealing with that person that caused the pain, often the person that caused the pain has been dead. Eons have passed and in essence you raise that person up and place them in a seat of prominence in your psyche thereby allowing bitterness to form a root well beyond what is normal for the present moment. This is the danger in unforgiveness. You are surrounded by demonic memories that have a vehicle to operate in this earth realm; YOU. You become the vehicle for the demonic forces of hell to traverse the earth.

The pain and memories began coming to a head at the passing of Norman McCleod. I went into autopilot and then walked away from God. I felt that He had let me down yet again, not knowing that He was maturing and preparing me through this man and his transition. I couldn't even understand what grieving was. I went into a tailspin downward into depression that I had never seen before. It was the culmination of things from my youth, military service, street experiences and now loneliness and fear. I sought treatment and discovered that not only was it a clinical diagnosis that was depression, but also an appearance of post-traumatic stress disorder of which I had not discussed with anyone from numerous events both civilian and military. I was a man! Men don't feel things like this! In treatment, I had to choose to go back to the original things in my life that caused me pain; of which I readily complied. Wise instruction was given to me that I may not remember all the painful things at will. And, I did not remember them all. But, other memories began to creep in once I destroyed the cap of selective memory and was honest! At times there are snippets of memories that come to give clarity to things. Instead of dwelling on them, I allow them to join to the event to give clarity and continually keep them all covered with forgiveness.

I was a man! Men don't feel things like this!

I went back to the earliest memory that I could think of; being potty trained. There I was in the bathroom; a small and narrow one much longer than it was wide. I was surrounded by my three sisters and my mother. I am standing with my little penis pointing to the water to relieve myself. When I finished urinating, I reached for a piece of toilet paper and wiped the tip of my little member. I was smacked with such speed for doing that! I had been made to accompany them to the bathroom while they relieved themselves and they wiped. I was only imitating what I witnessed. Now, I was really confused. I was told by one of them that boys don't wipe their "things". Well, what was the difference? And, did you wipe your "thing"? Don't we have the same "thing"? Not long after that, I remember my father often with such reluctance taking me to the toilet so I could learn to pee. Often times, he had to pee. I didn't. But, I went anyway and gained understanding of "aiming for the bubbles" in order to properly relieve myself as a man.

I have been told that the most effective way to change patterns that plague us is to face it, trace it, erase it and replace it.

It is in times like this that give us initial confusion which could also be a source of pain that we must bring forward to understand it. I have been told that the most effective way to change patterns that plague us is to face it, trace it, erase it and replace it. This is what I did. I faced the reason why I had a warped view about genitals for whatever purpose. I traced it to my initial experience concerning my own body. I erased it by understanding that the information and training given me was flawed from flawed sources. And, I replaced it by forgiveness, education and understanding. In turn, this began a healthy respect and understanding of sexual nature and my sexuality.

While many people, male and female, turn to other sexual lifestyles because of traumatic events, I chose to immerse myself in heterosexual promiscuity not realizing the reason why. As I sought the Lord concerning my behavior, He revealed that I was no different than one who chose a deviant lifestyle. The reasoning and consequence were there same! In addition, we have been programmed to view certain aspects of sexuality according to our upbringing.

While my upbringing was not necessarily Christian, any other deviance of sexuality was frowned upon. I will be brutally honest however. I saw no desire to embrace a man. I never wished to deviate, experiment or embrace anything but a woman although at times the woman may have been deviant apart from me. So, in being clear with society embracing the "ok" of deviant sexuality it is all not of God. Outside of the covenant of marriage there is no allowance for such activity. And, even then Biblically it is between a man and woman within the confines of marriage. Therefore, we are not to categorize any deviance from God's intention regardless of personal mindsets.

A reputation must be defended and maintained. A testimony is given for others to receive life.

So, in understanding "how" to overcome, we have two aspects. We have the Blood of the Lamb which has engrafted us into Christ. We have everlasting life because of the acceptance of His atoning sacrifice. But, even with that, we can live a defeated life as a Christian because of the refusal to give the "word of our testimony". Please remember the concept that will propel us further in deliverance, development and destiny. A reputation must be defended and maintained. A testimony is given for others to receive life. Give life that we may overcome.

Reflection

Do you fulfill the mandate of testifying of your life?

Do you wish to overcome or just be saved?

Who is your testimony for?

The Abundance of Obedience

So often we as men choose to put our experiences or presuppositions above the instructions of God. As my man of God often states (and his man of God as well), the anointing is in the instruction. One pericope of Scripture that I have always feasted upon in various ways is Luke 5:1-11.

'And it came to pass, that, as the people pressed upon him to hear the word of God, he stood by the lake of Gennesaret, saw two ships standing by the lake: but the fishermen were gone out of them, and were washing their nets. And he entered into one of the ships, which was Simon's, and prayed him that he would thrust out a little from the land. And he sat down, and taught the people out of the ship. Now when he had left speaking, he said unto Simon, Launch out into the deep, and let down your nets for a draught. And Simon answering said unto him, Master, we have toiled all the night, and have taken nothing: nevertheless at thy word I will let down the net. And when they had this done, they inclosed a great multitude of fishes: and their net brake. And they beckoned unto their partners, which were in the other ship, that they should come and help them. And they came, and filled both the ships, so that they began to sink. When Simon Peter saw it, he fell down at Jesus' knees, saying, Depart from me; for I am a sinful man, O Lord. For he was astonished, and all that were with him, at the draught of the fishes which they had taken: And so was also James, and John, the sons of Zebedee, which were partners with Simon. And Jesus said unto Simon, Fear not; from henceforth thou shalt catch men. And when they had brought their ships to land, they forsook all, and followed him."

If you want to find out if a man is prideful, insecure or both try to give him directions. There must be a gender-specific character flaw in us as men that we need to maintain control over being lost. Such is the same as Peter and his boys. They were functionally and professionally lost as to what to do and how.

We will continue to maintain that which worked in the past without giving thought to new equipment or actions.

They had done what they knew to do; fish. They had done it just like they did the night before as with every other night. Now, here comes this charismatic person talking to people that happened to be in close proximity for them to hear conversations. The people are really flocking to hear what He has to say. So, why not listen while we clean these same nets that are empty because we are using them the same as we always have? Yet, even though the same equipment is used, maybe we can just clean the nets and listen to this man. After all, they didn't have anything else to do. Now, that seems to be us as men at times. We will continue to maintain that which worked in the past without giving thought to new equipment or actions.

As they listened it sounded good! The people were really eating it up. But, they didn't go closer because they had to finish doing what they had been doing for quite some time. Now, there are times when we as men must be open to new ideas and functions. We cannot continually wash the same nets because it has produced historic results. God tells us to MOVE to another spot and try something that He is directing. But, if we are stuck on historical position and postures, we will never experience that move of God that we speak of and say that we desire.

Could it be that God is now pushing us into unknown functions and territories?

We tell people that God is moving, yet they see us within the same backdrop. We say that God is first in our lives. Yet, we want to listen to the other voices that direct us in another way. Could it be that God is now pushing us into unknown functions and territories? The Bible is filled with examples of God shifting someone to bless them. Both, Old and New Testament accounts always involve something that no one has heard of or done in the past. Could it be that we so ignorantly think that we have the mind of God?

When God says that He will do something new that means we don't know what it is. It's not new to God. It's new to man! We so ignorantly think that we have His mind. We don't. We are to have the mind of Christ. But, no one has the mind of the Father, but the Father. That's a simple truth that we have twisted. Christ even said that He only said what the Father said and did what the Father did. So, when the Father sends the Comforter to tell us something, it is new. We are now getting a download that was not with us before. So, we have to obey.

Peter and the boys could have questioned the authority of Jesus since He wasn't part of the fishing party. But, they acknowledged that something was different about this man. He taught with authority. He stood poised. The people were listening to Him as they pressed in. But, He was a carpenter. He wasn't a fisherman. That may pose the only problem. He didn't know anything (so they thought) about fishing. He may have been able to help them build a boat. But, He was not a fisherman!

The instruction was changed because this was a deep season, not shallow splashing!

It's amazing to me how Jesus just goes right to the person that has the influence; the one with the influence. He spoke directly to Peter; the one that most likely had everyone in step with an established. He told him to launch out into the deep. To me that makes much sense. It's daytime. The fish are in the deep. Yet, Peter answered Him from a place of historical failure. He said they had been fishing all night and caught nothing. Well, fish will come closer to shore at night to feed. The instruction was changed because this was a deep season, not shallow splashing!

How often do we as men answer the situation from past experiences or historical failure? Most likely we will continually answer our instructions with our own mindset as long as we are wise in our own sight. Through failed relationships, we answer the current instruction through our own pain. Through failed business ventures, we answer the current instruction through the last business model. Through financial struggles we answer the current situation through the last investment.

When God tells us to do something, go somewhere or say something, the obedience produces abundance.

Now Jesus tells them to go toss the nets in the deep water so they can get more fish than dreamed of. Why? Because, Jesus wanted them to be secure in following Him in ministry. He had to at least give them a three year salary and expense account for their families. When God tells us to do something, go somewhere or say something, the obedience produces abundance. I am well aware that society places the value on money instead of what money is exchanged for. Yet, as Christians, we must run from that mindset and put our focus on the Provider instead of the provisions.

This is the place that men need to be; a place of trust in God.

The Provider said to launch out into the deep. This was the beginning of the transition. This Carpenter said to go fishing. Go figure that one out. Andrew, James and John were no doubt watching to see what Peter would do. They would follow suit in turn. This was to set the stage for the complete three years. Peter would be the one who would be the spokesperson from this point out. Jesus had him pegged! Yet, Jesus didn't contend with him. This is the place that men need to be; a place of trust in God. We don't need to discussion, debate or reasoning with God. If He is saying it, then it's because He is sovereign; period.

The more bizarre an instruction coming from God may seem, the more bountiful the blessing.

Now, after all the bantering and historical recall, Peter launches into the deep and lets down the nets. The newly cleaned nets were now being dirtied again during the day when the fish were someplace enjoying the sunshine. I would have loved to be listening when they launched out. I can hear James and Andrew saying how Peter has bumped his head again. Yet, John may have been the one that sat back and observed for this time. He was positioning himself to be on the bosom of this Man. This Man was not like the rest that came through the docks with all kinds of messages.

Perhaps we need to take a lesson on this. The more bizarre an instruction coming from God may seem, the more bountiful the blessing. The image given for the fishing excursion is that of dragnets. It involves two boats with the nets being let down. They are then circled to catch the fish in the nets blocking any escape. It's quite ingenious. So, for them to accomplish this, they would have to maneuver both boats simultaneously.

This Man was not like the rest that came through the docks with all kinds of messages.

I think in a prophetic mindset. Boats have a representation of being a carrier of influence for many people. Therefore with two boats to me it is a representation of your natural and spirit man. Both aspects are to be used to corral the fish simultaneously; the symbol of provision and prosperity. Again, prosperity is not money, but provision, influence and sustenance. The net would represent the grasping of this need. The four men represent each corner of the earth that must give up the resources we as men need to be free from worry. And, finally in looking at the deep we see what is unknown. This is a place that someone beyond our understanding must provide us with details; instructions. This Person is God.

It is not wise to take risks without counsel. Therefore, we are to seek wise counsel. But, with the Mighty Counselor in their midst all the needed counsel was present! Therefore the only risk that was present was the risk of not taking the counsel. Our provision and abundance is wrapped up in our obedience.

The true representation of success is having experienced failure and trying again.

The misrepresentation of success is the absence of failure. I beg to differ from a popular mindset concerning success. The true representation of success is having experienced failure and trying again. Failure is the most integral part of success. Yet today no one will speak of the failures, often numerous ones that occur before success. Peter was already poised for success but was content dwelling in failure. We as men have been poised for success since birth. While I have your attention, we as Christian men need to understand that the failure of one man, Adam, positioned us with victory and success in Christ; success and victory already solidified before the foundation of the world.

Just at one word God can shift everything to a point that causes blessings to tackle us.

When we allow God to direct us into deep uncharted waters our success and abundance is well beyond affecting just us. Just as it did in this Gospel account, it will affect the prosperity and well-being of business partners, family, community and definitely the Kingdom of God. The net of containment will break because the provision of God will not be able to be contained. It matters not the political or economic climate. It only matters the spiritual temperature of your faith.

The awe at which God's presence and provision will touch our spirit will cause us to fall down at His feet in worship. Just at one word God can shift everything to a point that causes blessings to tackle us. He is attempting to free us from the madness associated with religion and allow us as men to receive fully everything needed. But, we must first take the word He gives us and launch out into the deep. Selah.

Reflection

Why are there blessings in your obedience?

Will your obedience bless others? How?

What will your obedience cost you? Why?

The Murderous Man

Such a title would bring many thoughts of various murders and the scenes. While all are true, there are many instances where modern society has attempted to dismiss some actions as not being murder. We can count sin as thought, word or deed. This is also true for criminal activity as well. In criminal activity the difference in punishment can be increased by virtue of premeditation if it is proven. Therefore our ability to murder someone can be thought out, spoken or carried out. While we as men often think that we have not committed any malicious murder if we didn't actually take a life, I beg to differ. If there has ever been a thought of how life would be different if a person died when there was no reason for that person's death, you have just murdered them mentally. If we have spoken a murderous word to someone such as "I wish you were dead", we have murdered. Even if you speak words not edifying concerning a person then they are murderous communications. And, certainly if you have murdered someone by taking their life, you have murdered. Men are known to speak much that would not edify one another. But, I would like to bring another aspect that is often ignored to our minds as men.

In today's society, we have allowed murderous men to go off stock free.

Biblically, when we think of murder immediately we often think of the Genesis account and that of Cain and Abel. Yet, even though this is also accepted as the first murderous account, it was not the first murder. The very first murder was in the Garden with Adam and Eve. The serpent had a thought, a word, and forced a deed causing malicious death. Satan murdered Adam and Eve, and therefore mankind. And in turn the murderous spirit remained in man to be passed down through the seed of Adam who was murdered. So, by the time it came to Cain, it was already strong with Abel being the first flesh to flesh murder victim and Cain being the first human perpetrator of such an act.

Men speak to authorize human sacrifice.

But, in today's society, we have allowed murderous men to go off stock free. How? Men speak to authorize human sacrifice. Again you ask how? They do it through abortion. This is not just a womanly crime of convenience or choice where we as men are not just as responsible if not more since we carry needed sperm seed. It takes two because a woman is not asexual. Yes, there are those instances where the man doesn't even know, even if he is married to the woman, her intentions concerning the child in the womb. But, I truly believe God will reveal this to him sooner or later. I ministered to a young man one time that was faced with the dilemma of not being able to stop his unborn child from being aborted. I prayed with him and declared that the child would not endure such a death. I instructed him that at all costs he must never speak it out of his mouth no matter what the argument. His words must never come into alignment with the act. As he stood on the truth and confessed God's word, the mother miscarried before arriving at the clinic for the act.

The child's nerves are formed and functional!

Yet, in more cases than enough, he does know and often initiates the perceived option that is really premeditation. He directs that this child be passed through the fires of Molech as recorded in 2 Kings 23:10. The child is a living child at the moment of conception and even before that physical point of birth, not when the child is born or gets his name and a birth certificate. The child is a child to come into this realm even before they arrive in the physical realm by conception. The Jeremiah account speaks to verifying this! Therefore, when the child is forced to be aborted, it is murder. Saint Augustine, an early authority in Christianity spoke vehemently against abortion which I found to be amazing seeing how today's church leaders don't make reference to early church fathers in this situation. I purposely have not quoted in hopes that we may obtain his works for our own reading enhancement. But, if this was the mindset in 400 C.E. then why has it changed now?

... Our immediate word is what counts.

In reference to murdering a child by allowing them to be offered to an idol, the sacrifice spoken of in 2 Kings 23:10 describes making your seed walk through fire. Most abortions performed at this time involve chemicals even saline solution which actually burns the child. The child is walking through fire in order to be aborted ending in death for most cases while feeling everything. The child's nerves are formed and functional! This is not to mention suction which tears the child's limbs apart and mutilates the child while being forcefully drawn from the uterus. There have been instances of children surviving this ordeal. While there is not much advertisement of this in the media, it does occur. Just find one of these survivors and you will witness a grace upon them so powerful until you will question why a person would even listen to an argument concerning this act.

We as men have been the party that has escaped most immediate judgment in such a thing; allowing the mothers to be the one to bear guilt and shame. But, God sees it! When the man discovers that he has brought forth life in any form, there is to be an immediate protection. Once the man says to "get rid of it" or agrees with the suggestion out of convenience and/or fear to abort the child, he is now a co-conspirator in the child's murder. I do acknowledge that he may not be informed of the pregnancy even if he is married. However, these are not the instances that I am addressing because he is ignorant of the action and the child's existence. I am addressing the willful suggestion and concurrence of murdering a child for the sake of deception, economical security or just plain inconvenience of parenthood. Yes, the woman is the one that has the final decision as whether or not to go through with it. But, our immediate word is what counts. If we say no to the discussion and decision of it, that may not be enough. There can be other pleading. And, in no cases if we have said no should we provide financial support, transportation or even physical presence to the act no matter what the emotional attachment. While many would say that this is being farfetched, I am not sure it is.

I am stepping directly into the face of men to take responsibility for our actions.

What if you said no to someone killing a neighbor then knowingly gives the person a ride after sitting in the living room or even the car while the murder is committed? Would not that be considered conspiracy and make you just as responsible? Then you give the person a ride home while comforting them in some perceived manner (nothing can erase what has occurred in the spirit of the person) after you have even possibly financed the murder. I don't think this is so farfetched when you put both of them together.

My brothers, many of us must repent for we have bought into the cultural norm that a fetus is not a "who", but an "it". Therefore, it is easier to annihilate an "it" that it is to murder a person. In the military, the first thing that is done when deploying troops to a combat area is to dehumanize the enemy to assist in killing him with ease. By any means necessary there is a name calling or the removal of identity from the enemy which makes it easier to take the life. This is the very same thing done to the child by dehumanizing the fetus in order to easily facilitate the murder and disposal of the body.

You are the escaped murderer who has to deceive himself in thinking that he did nothing wrong if he didn't make the decision.

I am not addressing women on this issue. There are other resources out there to assist her recovery from such actions that can be healed by going to God with a repentant heart. But, I am stepping directly into the face of men to take responsibility for our actions. We must repent and be honest as to not have protected the seed God entrusted us with. We must even have a period of grief concerning the loss. Without going into details fully, I personally have two instances to grieve for. In both, I had no other way to stop what was occurring. Yet, in one I sheepishly and ignorantly gave transportation to and from the procedure. While I vehemently spoke my disdain, I provided the transportation which negated my words! I don't forget either and think of what they would have been now as adults; my seed. My only peace is that I am forgiven by God, and that they child has been in His presence. There was no justification of possible birth defects or danger to the mother or her life. It was a choice made in order to free the mother from the responsibility. In the end, what was thought to bring us closer drove me apart in such a way as to never look back again. Yet, this comfort cannot be given until there is a confession to the sin of abortion which is murder and very possibly sexual immorality.

If you did not vote for a godly and God-fearing civic leader on any level, then you have contributed as well.

So my brothers, don't even feel that it's the woman that must bear the burden. You are the escaped murderer who has to deceive himself in thinking that he did nothing wrong if he didn't make the decision. I am forward with this because we have collectively as men helped destroy our nation which this along with helping to make the wombs of our women barren. Let it sink in. If you don't agree, that is your prerogative. But, when you don't agree you must have some justification in mind. You ask how you contributed if you have not been in concert with a pregnancy. If you did not vote for a godly and God-fearing civic leader on any level, then you have contributed as well. I don't agree with men **not** being jointly responsible for abortion. Even if you are married and there was an abortion, the question is asked as to why didn't the wife inform you? If it was an adulterous relationship, then you are involved as well as not providing some need to leave a door open, even if it was a perceived need and couldn't be provided. If it was one conceived out of the marital relationship, then you were involved and she had some reasoning for not telling you. Either way, we as men are just as guilty for abortions that we allowed. We must confess and repent immediately for our sin and the sins of those associated with us!

Reflection

Who have you sentenced to death with your words or actions?

How can you prevent murder in the Body of Christ?

Will you commit to removing the death sentence from your mouth?

The Art of Concealment

It is quite an interesting concept when you can be in a place and not be detected as your true identity. That is true concealment. Men have become masters at concealment! We cover ourselves totally and blend in with expectations and desires. We blend in for the expectation that we are macho and suave only to be in reality a child with a mask on or a person with so many gaping wounds that we should be dead. We blend in with concealment to be the suave man of the hour only to mask the multiple insecurities we have. So what do we do? We practice social, financial and spiritual penis envy. We secretly admire and despise what another is doing while we continue to conceal our own identity behind the layers of whatever can be used to blend in.

We blend in with concealment to be the suave man of the hour only to mask the multiple insecurities we have.

Now, before we begin to beat our chests in denial let's get real with the mirror and the model that provides the image. I won't even begin in society because that's where we are first given this problem. We can begin in the church; yes church! We have been bamboozled to think that there is some hierarchy to serving which would boost our falsely perceived importance. In essence we begin acting like little kids that have something better, bigger or faster than those around us. Our insecurity shows when we must be 'better' than our brother or be in a perceived more elevated position. Even when a brother says that he doesn't really care about being 'up there' can be saying in essence that he is in a better position than all who compete. And, he may very well be! But, what matters is "how" he serves, not where he serves.

Our insecurity shows when we must be 'better' than our brother or be in a perceived more elevated position.

I give an example as a janitor. He cleans and ensures the cleanliness of all aspects of the ministry building(s). If he succumbs to the mindset that it's all about him and he can never be replaced, he has just fallen victim to the art of concealment. While it may not look like much to others, to God it still is pride. Brothers beware. You can be replaced by God at any given moment according to His will. And, your replacement may be by someone who has a smidgen at most of the qualifications you possess. They only possess one qualification; to love God.

Brothers, think about how we go to great lengths to fit in with our mannerisms and fashions. We may say that we are "the original" while only being a clone of another fashion or social trend. I grew up in the era of the Afro, bell bottom trousers with platform heel shoes. I am convinced that the explosion of orthopedic surgeons was spawned from the stack heel era and all the orthopedic damage we inflicted on our limbs. Our feet, our knees and our ankles suffered for the sake of fashion. Even in church, we are expected to be of a certain "look" in order to be accepted into the unconditionally loving family of God. Well, that is such malarkey. If you don't believe that statement, show up in church wearing anything that is not religiously accepted. Show up in a predominately Black church wearing a Klu Klux Klan jacket or a predominately White church wearing a "kill the racist pig" t-shirt. I'm sure the deacon board will not need a meeting to approach you. Yet, this is what we inadvertently teach; hypocrisy. We will accept you if you look like us. Language has not even been deployed yet. The sense of hearing is not in effect, only sight. And, if sight is not satisfied, then hearing is full of static.

Even in church, we are expected to be of a certain "look" in order to be accepted into the unconditionally loving family of God.

The first act of concealment was in the Garden of Eden. While we look at Eve as the one and only culprit and try to paint Adam as the victim, we don't think of whom it was that ordered the concealment. Eve had only come lately on the scene and was designed to help Adam. Until that fateful moment Adam had been the one that was tending the garden; knowing each and every plant and the functions of them. When Eve turned and gave to her husband the historical, juicy and fateful bite immediately when they saw there were naked the minds needed concealment. They went into the design business quickly with Adam leading and managing the production.

Yet, to take a pause on our concealment issue, I want to produce some food for thought. The Bible records that they made aprons to cover themselves. Why is it that when we think of nakedness only the genitals come to mind. Men, we are doubly guilty of this only thinking that the one region of our body constitutes nakedness. In essence our whole body is naked if our mind is not covered. God had to cover them with "tunics" made from the skin of an animal. A tunic covers more than just the frontal privates as depicted in art. The tunic also covers the heart; a very vital place of our spiritual existence. Could it have been that God was attempting to preserve us in that skins are more weather worthy for the storms of life than leaves? In addition our minds were not covered with the skins. Why? It was because we have to allow our minds to be covered with the proof of Blood. Our senses were not covered or restricted. We used all of them except smell in order to reject God in pride. Only the sense of smell was not used in the initial fall. However, in the redemption, smell had to be used. Never had Adam smelled blood. Now, he could smell with the skin of the Lamb that was slain from the foundation of the world. Now, we know what sin smells like; a stench that must be experienced to be eradicated.

In essence our whole body is naked if our mind is not covered.

I have heard my pastor give a very graphic teaching on the penis and vagina and the similarities of them being indicative of the high priest and the Temple. It was so graphic with the anointing of God until where I watched the same young women that were coming into the college Bible study for other reasons whether religious or social leave changed; resolved. While they passed the pool room on the way in with smiles at the available guys on the tables, the passed on the way out with another outlook! Many times I have read, re-read and read again the passages in Genesis. I could never see where it is recorded what level of concealment they attempted to obtain. But, if we can logically think on the subject, they were trying to hide from an omniscient and omnipotent God. Therefore a fig leaf would not be sufficient. Yet, to sew many together may make them appear in their own eyes as trees of righteousness, but not to God. Perhaps this is what Isaiah reference when he was inspired to write of us becoming trees of righteousness. And, I am sure that Adam was the designer. So perhaps we need to allow them both to be mentioned instead of giving Eve center stage on the Fall. That was a powerful attempt at concealment.

In the military, concealment meant survival. When you are properly concealed the enemy cannot easily locate you. In order to be properly concealed we must be hidden in Christ, not in church. We have so many hiding places. Yet those places involve much of what we are using to cover us; temporal things. You can hide in riches. But, what happens when money or tangible riches no longer provide the cover and concealment they once did? We even try to conceal ourselves in religious camouflage while knowing the complete time that we have no intention on conforming to the image of Christ.

Therefore, since we are in combat, we are to be concealed totally in Christ. When the enemy sees Christ, he can't see us. Yet, he knows we are somewhere in Him. We are clothed in His righteousness not our own design. This is what we should remember when we feebly attempt to clothe our ego and existence with the things in which we conceal ourselves. I won't go into such detail, but we know what they are. Our concealment has been in the form of clothing, sports, cars, degrees, organizations or fraternities, the gymnasium, women and even "church". Yes, we even try to conceal ourselves in religious camouflage while knowing the complete time that we have no intention on conforming to the image of Christ.

When you are properly concealed the enemy cannot easily locate you. Therefore

Therefore, we need a new direction in life. I recommend instead of concealing ourselves and slinking through life like a sniper getting into position to engage the next intended target which may be another brother, why not go another way? Why not just get naked and allow God to clothe us in His righteousness? Our attempts were short lived and limited in purpose compared to the covering provided by the Lord. This is the only way that our concealment will be sufficient to hide us in all aspects of our meager existence without Him. Then when someone sees what you are clothing yourself in, they will only know there is only one place to get that covering; the Lamb of God. Selah.

Reflection

Will you stop concealing yourself and be transparent?

What methods have you used in concealment?

What reality did you attempt to portray?

Using Your Manly Authority as a Shield of Defense

As Christian men we embrace the thought and often misconception that people come to Christ through the church because they are hurting in some manner. Whether they are hurting from crisis that has befell them or just because they understand that they cannot attain the level of perfection that others have told them they should have makes no difference. However, when they arrive what do they find? Do they find others that have come in, but not changed their clothes? Do they find others that by virtue of longevity have been made leaders who never had to deal with their own issues? As a seminarian (and truly it is not a point of boasting) I observed many that produced doctrine based on concealing their own shortcomings or issues. They were determined to formulate a congregation to where they would never be hurt again. Many were determined to form their own "Never Never Land" where every day was Super Bowl Sunday bringing endless snacks and entertainment. I realized that before anyone attempts to walk into ministry or even study theology to present to anyone including themselves there must be counseling along with true accountability to a PERSONAL pastor. There must be a personal one on one relationship with accountability. If there is not, the issues in your back pocket will be presented to those with a hand out for life designed and established by your own experiences and expectations of congregational life.

So often we don't allow the grace to be extended to others that we extend to ourselves.

I have experienced this as well and no doubt have injured others out of ignorance. But, with the grace of God and the honesty of allowing the Holy Spirit to be able to continually (not just a one-time shot) point out areas of correction in your life we grow in grace. So often we don't allow the grace to be extended to others that we extend to ourselves. We try to rationalize the distribution of grace. But, when I find someone that only criticizes or judges other Christians while minimizing or excusing their own humanity I withdraw to prayer. If there is any correction however gentle often it is deemed to be an attack instead of an act of love toward the person. We take correction as an attack and at best unnecessary rebuke. Think of the example of a man with his zipper open. A brother approaches him and says, "My brother you need to check yourself". The man can flip out and storm away. Then he walks down a street and everyone is giggling. Then a mentally challenged homeless woman walks up to him and says in a loud voice among mid-day shoppers, "your underwear reminds me of my last three lovers; full of stripes and surprises". Now, this man who didn't properly receive correction has received humiliation at the expense of a challenged woman's fantasy! This is the process that we overlook; loving rebuke.

We hide behind a title or function all the while keeping our little boy pain hidden.

We become leaders and then we take the hurt with us. We hide behind a title or function all the while keeping our little boy pain hidden. In listening to a sermon by Apostle Anthony Wallace he presented the following rhema to us:

> *"Some leaders don't know that they are hurting. And, whenever you are a leader, it's easy to build a place of structure; a place of however you want to build it because you have that capacity....don't make your place of authority a place of defense, that you fight from..."*

We men are leaders! Yet, we move to that place where we build the defense of manhood not realizing that it has been manned by a little boy scared to venture out of the fort of perceived safety. We especially need to present our true self to another man for accountability and not the reasonable facsimile. We need to present the good, bad, ugly, hidden and disguised. In this manner we can be guided into the will of God by an objective person. Now, if you choose to find only those who will coddle you and be an affirmation to your idiotic mentality, you have just been granted the permission and passage to become the world's biggest fool. You have not moved into progression but into stagnation. In stagnant water nothing has life unless it is for the purpose of bringing sickness and death. Foul odors instead of a sweet fragrance; insects instead of fish and birds; all this will be the backdrop of the garbage of insecurity, fear and pride that have been dumped thereby never allowing life to perpetuate in your waters of life.

We need to present the good, bad, ugly, hidden and disguised.

Brothers, allow other men to help you clean out your cesspool and restore it to being a cistern of life; an oasis teeming with life. Only then will you welcome other life and be a blessing to the relationships that other life brings; reciprocal life. We must come out of hiding as leaders. We are leaders in some right somewhere within life. We must allow others to see our humanity and frailty so we can contribute that frailty to the deliverance and progression of others. It is a reason that John recorded on Patmos that we are delivered not only by the Blood of the Lamb, but also by the word of our testimony. A testimony cannot be a testimony unless another hears it. Otherwise, it isn't a testimony, it is only self-talk which is good for nothing but convincing ourselves of what we think of ourselves; positive or negative. We must immediately stop attempting to mask the bonfires or our past. Why? We must stop it because they are actually beacons of hope and life for others to make it to shore and begin again. Selah!

Reflection

How many times have you used your "man card" to defer from addressing a painful or needed situation?

How often do you hide your emotions from your spouse or significant other, other men or even your pastor because it may tarnish your "manhood"?

How will you begin to become transparent?

Forgiveness
(The Biggie)

The most dangerous sin that a man can commit will never be murder. It will be suicide. I am not saying that a man will physically kill himself. I am saying that he will spiritually kill himself which will lead ultimately into a physical, psychological and emotional death. As we harbor unforgiveness in any form in our hearts we have choked the very essence of our existence out of our lives: God Himself.

Men often hold the warrior mentality over the meekness requirement.

God is very adamant in His word concerning unforgiveness. If we do not forgive everyone, neither can He forgive us! I found it very interesting to note that He did not make any stipulations on whether or not the person was saved by His Son's sacrifice or just a plain heathen. He just says forgive in order that we may be forgiven. Therefore, those people that don't go to your church and wronged you must be immediately forgiven. I have had to practice this principle of immediate and spontaneous forgiveness so many times with family, society, employment and even in the church.

We were never designed to be lone rangers.

We are not limited to a specific realm of society in which we forgive. As a matter of fact, we are to practice the agape or God kind of love continuously toward all people. This is not to say that you willingly allow someone to continuously hurt you or your family. In no way would I espouse such a belief. And, I would strongly attack any doctrine that espoused this mentality. Men often hold the warrior mentality over the meekness requirement. Meekness is never to be considered weakness. It is to be considered you being submissive to God and keeping your natural power under control. This is where forgiveness comes in.

We should know beyond a shadow of a doubt where at least one other man is in all of his existing states; spiritually, emotionally and psychologically.

You as a man actually have the power to kill yourself and others. You can kill yourself spiritually if you are not connected to the Holy Spirit who will teach you all things. He would quickly convict you of your unforgiveness. However, you have the power over Him to reject forgiveness and choose, unwisely, to harbor unforgiveness thereby killing yourself spiritually. It is much harder to harm yourself physically because we are innately equipped with safety mechanisms to survive. However, with our spiritual, emotional and psychological being we are able to harm ourselves often without realizing it. This is why we need other men to watch over us, warning us of impending danger.

When Cain so rudely answered God in Genesis 4:9, he was actually presenting a truth to us. Yes, we are our brother's keeper. We should know beyond a shadow of a doubt where at least one other man is in all of his existing states; spiritually, emotionally and psychologically. We are keepers one to another. When God asks me about my accountability brother(s) then I must be able to give an account for them just as they must give an account for me! We were never designed to be lone rangers. We were designed to be relational. And, we can never be relational without being forgiving. Even if the pain is still there and fresh, we are to still forgive. The quicker you forgive, the less damage you will inflict upon your spirit.

Be careful for your reasons of attending church my brothers. Works will not qualify you for God's approval.

On a personal testimony, I harbored things from my youth against family members that had wronged me greatly. However, as I realized in maturation how much those things were destroying me in more ways than one, I cried out like the apostles to the Lord. I needed the demonstration of more faith to forgive! I had given my life to the Lord accepting Him as my Savior first then Lord. Yet, there were these "things" that would pop up in my mind. I can't even call them memories because they were consuming! They would pop up as I was reading the Bible, thinking on the things of God or just out of the blue when I was still. I had learned how to pray according to the examples before me; often no more than rote repetitions. I attended church regularly as if that alone would qualify me for heaven. (Be careful for your reasons of attending church my brothers. Works will not qualify you for God's approval.) I wanted to truly live for God. Yet, these "things" kept me in a state of despair and anger.

I made it the top priority of my life to find where pockets of unforgiveness were hiding and cleaning them out.

After experiencing things in the military that were traumatic to me, I remember telling a psychologist that my problem was spiritual and not psychological. What a rhema that was. I remember him really thinking I was truly crazy! I could never have said that on my own wisdom. As it turned out this was the truth. My problem was spiritual in root yet psychological in manifestation! The wrong of abuse in many forms done to me in many instances and fashions threatened to weaken the foundation that I was laying as sand would weaken concrete. It took a very hard look into the Word of God to see that if I did not forgive, He could not, (He didn't say would not but could not) forgive me! I made it the top priority of my life to find where pockets of unforgiveness were hiding and cleaning them out. As I began to trace it back to my childhood, peeling away things like an onion, I began forgiving all from family members, community people, religious authorities and anyone else that had wronged me in any fashion.

Then I was guided by the Lord to take it one step further; PRAY FOR THEM. Huh? Do what? Yes, pray for those who have offended you in any way. You cannot hate who you pray for with the agape love of God. A very good way for me to pray for them was to think of sin as all encompassing. If I stole a paper clip and wasn't forgiven by the Blood of the Lamb, I was just as guilty as a mass murderer. I imagined being in hell next to all the mass murderers in eternity. They would scream in pain saying they wish they hadn't killed all the people and not repented. I was screaming just as loud in eternity wishing I had left the paper clips on the desk and repented while I had the chance. It was a sobering thought.

While I forgave, I began to look at other examples of forgiveness. I reviewed many to record in this writing. However, one stood out above all else; one that there is no comparison in my recollection. A young woman in our congregation received news that her father, an elderly man and well respected by his community, had been brutally murdered. His reputation was one of sterling character and he was filled with compassion. There would was no connection to anything awry in his life; only praise for how he stood highly esteemed in the community. While there was grieving in her emotions, the one thing that stood out among all things was her concern for the souls of those responsible for the hideous crime. Her requests for prayers were not just for the grieving family members, but of the souls and well-being of the ones responsible. She openly prayed that they would know she forgave them and that other family members would be moved in the love of God to quickly do the same; never to seek any iota of revenge. Her prayer included massive intercession that they would accept Christ as Lord and Savior. I was so touched to see her sincere desire concerning forgiveness. She displayed to a congregation of more than a few how God was working in her concerning true forgiveness.

I noticed that the disciples in Luke 17 (*again I purposely leave out verses to encourage reading of the complete chapter*) asked Jesus to increase their faith. I may not have really given this a Selah moment except that it came on the heels of Him teaching concerning forgiveness. It is nothing but faith that can be used to forgive someone in any instance. And, then with me witnessing the young woman forgiving in such a way immediately following her receiving the heinous news really drove this Scripture home in my spirit. What she did at that moment was to allow me to go all the way back in my memory and see how many times I didn't forgive someone and the pain it caused me; not them. While I had learned the lesson and obeyed the instruction from the Word of God, this instance gave me a practical example of the power of forgiveness; no hesitancy just instant forgiveness. And, then the blessing in the form of praying for not against the perpetrators while binding other family members from harming them was nothing other than the power of God at work.

God places those people with His grace in front of us to be the examples that we should seek to model.

This is an example that every man needs to follow since the warrior spirit can and will rise up in us with a quickness to extract revenge in the form of perceived justice. It is a forgiveness like that that emanated from her spirit immediately upon notice that we must emulate at all times regardless of what the infraction. In a reflective moment, I shudder at what my first thought would have been. Yet, God places those people with His grace in front of us to be the examples that we should seek to model.

God never said that He would "forget" anything.

Since our most deadly form of self-destruction is unforgiveness, then we must ensure that we forgive not only quickly but completely regarding nothing of the offense in our heart. I will never say to forgive and forget, nor attempt to drop that nonsense in the form of stating it is said in the Bible. God never said that He would "forget" anything. He said that he would "remember" our sins no more. In other words, He will not "re" (make over again) "member" (put together) our sin since we have confessed (agreed with God on the matter) our sin to Him and He has forgiven us. I am not saying that all the consequences of sin are wiped away. Never would I say such a thing. There are instances where no physical or seen consequences are observed. However, there will always be a spiritual or unseen consequence; the constant reminder of our deserved fate and guilt. Now, just as He has done with us, we are to do with others. Otherwise, we are still covered in our own sin.

PAUSE!

AT THIS POINT RELEASE YOURSELF BY BEGINNING TO WRITE A HEARTFELT LETTER OF RECALL AND FORGIVENESS TO THAT PERSON OR PERSONS WHO HAVE CAUSED YOU PAIN OR INJUSTICE. THEN CONTINUE ON. IF IT IS A FAMILY MEMBER THAT IS STILL ALIVE ENSURE THAT YOU ACKNOWLEDGE WHAT EFFECT THIS HAS HAD ON YOUR EXISTENCE AND ASK FOR THEIR FORGIVENESS. WHY? MOST LIKELY YOU NEED FORGIVENESS.

Write in detail. You have the next few pages to express yourself.

Then continue.

Dear _____

Reflection

How quickly do you forgive someone?

Is it hard for you to forgive yourself?

Can you accept forgiveness as an act of grace; needing nothing more than acceptance? If not, why not?

Bodily Connection

I have often heard many men state that they are connected to God and don't need to go to church. Well, I won't offer a theological discourse concerning this, but a natural one. It is evident that God has used many natural things to teach us spiritual concepts. One of the concepts is that of abiding in the vine. Now, why would He use a vine to teach us a concept concerning Himself Who is all-encompassing? Well, first of all, we are not God, and need to be connected to a life source. When we are mavericks out in the world "doing me" as so many would inaccurately state their actions in life, we have nothing to sustain us. You can only "do you" but for so long before you will be done with you! It is in this instance that proof of our need to be connected to God is evident.

You can only "do you" but for so long before you will be done with you!

I spent much of my life "doing me" in which I found out that I had no clue concerning who "me" really was. I connected to so many sources until I wasn't even sure what attachment to use to fully receive the functional power from the source. Too often I had the wrong connection and the wrong energy flowing through me. There was nothing wise or settled about what "me" was. This is the beginning of me reaching back to those "things" I had learned about God. Unfortunately, many of the fallacies or idiotic theological doctrines obtained from various ignorant sources were intermingled. Yet, through it all, His truth constantly would surface to the top. It is here that I could reason with worldly wisdom that there needed to be a connection.

When a man does not want to be connected to anything, I wonder where the hidden pain is.

As a young youth, I joined the military. In basic training, you were always told to stay connected to your buddy; the one in your bunk area. That was the one that regardless of what you felt about him, you were stuck for at least eight weeks. Unfortunately, I had someone that was a true walking hemorrhoid. Yet, I survived the eight weeks then moved on. I would be amiss in admitting that at the end of the eight weeks, he wasn't such a pain as I had envisioned, just different from me. As a matter of fact I even acknowledged to him that I was probably more of a pain to him than he was to me. We actually became great friends and connected again at my first duty station. Alas, my world was expanding even in the midst of mental, physical and culinary anguish associated with basic training in the military.

I do understand the instances where parents may not be the ideal connection, yet we arrived here by them.

Growing up in an urban area, you understood the importance of not being a maverick. You knew that you must be connected to someone, even if it was only for selected reason. Whether it be a true gang or a group of people that associated and hung out on a regular basis, connection was vital. Then there is the familial unit. You are connected to parents; period. I do understand the instances where parents may not be the ideal connection, yet we arrived here by them. What happened after that is in the hands of God. However, no child came to this earth without a mother and father regardless of what goes on after their arrival. Those two genders got them here. So, we do see there must be a connection.

If the fruit on the vine is not connected to the vine which is connected to the root as the root is in the source they all die.

How is it that when it concerns God we wish to be alone? One of the names of God is *Elohim*, the plural form of *El* which means *Strong One*. The name alone represents relationship and connection. I have heard it said sadly too often that a man doesn't need to go to church to worship God. Well, yes you do. Again, the vine has a root. If the vine is not rooted, it dies. If the fruit on the vine is not connected to the vine which is connected to the root as the root is in the source they all die. Yet, with such a simplistic example, we decide that we know better than God when we rebel against this. I often wonder how God just looks at us shaking His head saying, "I gave them the simplest example that I could, yet they choose to be dumber than a bag of hammers thinking they know more than Me!" From the very beginning, destruction of connection was what began the death scenario. So, in our original fellowship with God, we were connected!

Pride tells man that He can do better than God.

When a man does not want to be connected to anything, I wonder where the hidden pain is. Where did he hide the "thing" or "things" that have wounded him where he is hiding from every aspect of connection? Did he ever address the issues that cause him to be solitary? If he can't be connected to God, how can he be connected to anything else? God has everything in His hand? How does he connect in relationships; marital, familial and social? There are many questions to be answered. But, the answer to all of these questions can be rooted in two aspects; pain and pride. This is as plain as it gets. Pride tells man that He can do better than God. And, the pain that caused the anesthetic pride is still festering within.

This is what happens to lives apart from Him; rotting before death.

I do understand that some relationships are not connective and would not try to encourage some to be forced, even familial ones. But, in the relationship with God, there is no way that you will continue to grow and prosper without

Him. His grace is so wondrous in that He even allows us to continue to exist apart from Him for a time, often a very long time constantly wooing us to Him. But, as with the fruit on the vine, if it is not connected to a source of life, it rots and dies. This is what happens to lives apart from Him; rotting before death. And, for those who think that it is all a farce, your body is continually rotting, but your soul will live on along with your spirit in eternal death at the Great White Throne of judgment.

A final example may be more convincing of the need to connect to a house of faith and submission to a Godly Pastor. I was blessed (although at the time I didn't see it) to have a grandfather who was a farmer. So, I did learn quite a bit about agriculture and animal husbandry; as much as a summer agricultural implant could. On the agriculture side, I could watch the peach trees in the yard yield their fruit along with the tomatoes and other fruit.

One thing that I noticed was that as long as the fruit was attached to the branch or grapes to the vine, they were ever so juicy and alive. If the fruit fell to the ground, it may be a day or so but rotting began. The insects and other animals would eat it. The sun began to extract all the fluids from it. The dirt from the ground began to claim its skin. In essence, it was dying quickly. However, there was a chance for the next tree, vine or plant to sprout in the form of the seed. Eventually, all of us will return to the earth. But, there is no need to rush it. I say that to say this. The only thing that I saw of a lasting timeframe on the ground was a nut. That could lie on the ground for quite a long time before it was absorbed into the earth and also began another life. Brothers, don't be a nut. Enjoy being above ground as fruit so all can see and taste. Selah

Reflection

How many times have you out of frustration or outright rebellion said that you were going to do it the way you wanted; in essence to "do you"?

How long can you stay apart from connections and think you flourish?

If there is a truthful look into connections, which connections have you severed to maintain a toxic one? Why?

Mutual Submission

Someone once pointed out to me in a chauvinistic manner that the Bible said the woman was the weaker vessel. And, as many theological doctrines that are perpetuated go, I never went to investigate this on my own. I took their dictation as face value. But, as the years passed and I began to experience more in life, I noticed something. Women were not as weak as men in many areas. I watched as children were born. The agony of the mother giving birth is something bizarrely supernatural! This woman is writhing and screaming in pain where a "human" is exiting her in a channel that has to stretch well beyond the girth of what impregnated her! And, then she is "normal" again seeking to hold this now living pain and lovingly nurture the child!

Women were not as weak as men in many areas.

I personally am glad that the Lord saw fit for me to be a man. I don't think I would consider marriage after understanding the pain in the loss of virginity. Then to hopefully have my painful loss of virginity be followed with my body being "joyfully" deformed while awaiting excruciating pain that is called a bundle of joy. I think being in a secluded order of some sort may not have been so bad considering all of this. But, yet, we think we are ultra-strong and able to endure all.

The beauty of the internet presented a clip with men who were made to carry pseudo pregnancies and experience labor through technology. The men chosen had wives who were in fact pregnant. In the experiment they could not handle the pain even close to labor that an expectant mother experiences. Again, I say this is truly supernatural. And, as I think of women who are in labor for many hours, I am humbled that my mother endured this not once, but many times! Again, my residence would have been littered with convent living brochures had I been a woman with this present mindset.

The most pain that we will endure is that of submission.

While this is but one aspect of what we do not have to endure as a man, there is another aspect that appears to be more painful; submission. The most pain that we will endure is that of submission. Somehow we think that submission is a sign of weakness without logically understanding the word. In order for someone to submit, there has to be a possibility of equal or more power. But, in our minds somehow we don't think that submission is powerful in itself. This is so far from the truth. Even in our submission to the Lord, we are turning over all of the power He actually gave us back to Him! Imagine that. The most powerful Being in any thought of imagination turning over power to resist Him to us; His creation. Then with His power turned over to us in this aspect of His being, He becomes submissive to us in allowing us to turn that power back over to Him that He may wondrously bless us. Yet too often we only give Him limited power to influence our lives. We think we still need to be in control of it. My mind cannot fathom the fullness of this example of submission by God to us.

In order for someone to submit, there has to be a possibility of equal or more power.

Our refusal to submit is extended in our relationships; choosing who we may submit to and the instances of such submission. I have been guilty of this as well, especially in the marriage covenant. Out of ignorance I thought I had it all going on in the world that I thought I lived in. I was wrong; desperately wrong. I had listened to others misquote out of context that the wife is to be submissive to her husband; not reading past the comma where she is actually submitting to the husband as if she submitted to the Lord. God's directive order was established not pecking order. But, until I decided that there was too much going wrong in my marriage and decided to really dig into it, I went right along with the ignorance. Then something wonderful happened. I actually read the Bible for myself instead of allowing man to tell me what God said when God was right there with me! I discovered the verse that was so often misquoted and looked one verse up!

In the pericope of Ephesians 5:21-31, God speaks to us concerning Christ and the church although He uses marriage as an example. All of this is relayed to us through the writings of the Apostle Paul. Now, in the submitting one to another tells us that this is not just related to the marriage relationship. It is related to life in general. Those who are in our community deserve a level of submission as well as those in our familial units. How is it that we submit to a stranger, politicians, police, teachers, doctors and even pastors, but we will not submit to each other? It makes no sense. And, we as men are to lead the way in submission beginning with God, our spouses and moving forward as He directs. If we as men say we do not submit to anyone, I dare them to call the Internal Revenue Service to inform them of your refusal to pay taxes. When you disconnect from that call, place another call to the Secret Service and inform them that regardless of what they say you are coming to stay at the White House tonight. When that is finished then you run the red light as the policemen are in their car monitoring the traffic. Then we can see that while you think you have not submitted by all these actions, you will be placed in a submission "hold" until you are placed in a holding tank to be forced into submission by the law. So let's begin total submission to God and then to our families. The community will follow us in the example we give. Selah.

Reflection

What has influenced your current view concerning the submission of women?

Have you taken the time to understand submission and the power behind it?

If you have submitted and experienced pain have you forgiven that person? Was it that you may have wrongly submitted to erroneous doctrine; especially in religious circles?

The Kingdoms of Existence

As we began to grow into our existence we may have been told very little about God, His Kingdom and our place in it. But, as men it is our responsibility to search out these things because it will define our existence on this earth. Yet, too many think that faith or the issues of spirituality are for another and not for us. This is why at various times in our lives we begin to gravitate toward a spiritual awakening that is often warped, perverted and ultimately detrimental to our spiritual life. I say this because every person gravitates toward spirituality regardless of what aspect it is. Whether it is fraternal organizations, church organizations or even social justice stances, they all begin in the spiritual arena. Even if the person speaks of the foolishness of being an atheist, it still is gravitation toward spirituality in order to fight the reality of it.

Man is a spirit, and will still reach toward things of some spirit even if not the Most High; Yahweh. Even our gravitation toward God can be warped in that we have been slothful by allowing others to define the God of our creation. Our quest to find God is shaped by our understanding often given to us in error of Who He truly is. I can recall having a conversation with a scientist of the mind that could not explain God. Therefore, since he couldn't explain God, he attempted to reduce Him to some pie-in-the-sky creature that we could haphazardly go to when we needed a magical fix to a problem. In addition, he actually tried to say that God was the outlet of a weak person's uncertainty about everyday life. I recall telling him if the person actually was reaching outside to another entity then there had to be a possibility of existence. He then tried to backtrack from the issue. But, logically, I would not reach down to pick up a penny unless there is a possibility of a penny being on the sidewalk. Correct? But, who was I? After all, he was a scientist of the mind according to his own description.

We spout the religious clichés concerning God's Kingdom not understanding the dimensions of it.

Let me be very clear. Kingdom citizenship and Christianity are not for chumps. If you cannot give a person the reason for the hope that you have and defend your faith, then there is a problem. You have to move your own feelings out of the way and be bold as a lion yet gentle as a lamb. I once heard someone say that sometimes you have to touch a person with a velvet glove over an iron hand. I prefer a loving touch over a strong grip. But, either way, it is not for chumps and the faint of heart especially in today's times.

While God is Creator over all, He has allowed until the appointed time rule to remain in certain areas of creation.

The main issue is that we have no idea of our citizenship in the Kingdom of our Lord. We spout the religious clichés concerning God's Kingdom not understanding the dimensions of it. Just as there are two realms, natural and spiritual. While God is Creator over all, He has allowed until the appointed time rule to remain in certain areas of creation. Yet, we can choose to move from one kingdom to another; from this world's system to the Kingdom of God or Heaven. While others may speak of the difference in two kingdoms and attempt to discredit Biblical writings because of the two names, there is still one King. I can call Britain, England. And, I can call the United States of America, America. These titles are interchangeable.

Whether it is the Kingdom of God or the Kingdom of Heaven, you must figure that out. The titles can be interchangeable and were recorded as so depending on the audience being addressed. For the sake of time we shall just speak of the Kingdom of God as an inclusive kingdom. But, in order to fully understand and reap the benefits of any citizenship, one must first become a citizen or be born into the kingdom. Far too often men settle for the vagabond or wandering spirit; never belonging to a residential kingdom. Yet, if you are not of the Kingdom of God, then by default you are of the kingdom of darkness. You cannot have citizenship in a kingdom of dusk to dawn. Either it is light or dark. But, we want to split hairs. This mentality is likened to being almost pregnant. Either you are or you are not!

I have been on the receiving end of bad treatment of some sort because of my beliefs.

As an American citizen, I am bound by the laws and some traditions of my country. Yet, there are some customs, laws and traditions that I deem against the Word of God and will not even participate in to the point of civil disobedience. It is not that I will not be a citizen anymore. It is that my identity in Jesus Christ forbids me to "sell out" to what man deems is more important than God's order. There is a price to pay. I have been on the receiving end of bad treatment of some sort because of my beliefs. Yet, as in standing as a man of God and not just a civil vagabond floating from culture and belief to the next for the sake of belonging I find peace. It is not a judgmental aspect. It is a choice.

"NICOTINE: HARDER TO KICK...THAN HEROIN" dated March 29, 1987 in the New York Times it is a monster to stop.

Take smoking for instance. While it is not illegal to smoke and nicotine is readily available, it is my choice not to be around it. I do understand the euphoric and addicting feeling that it brings. I also understand that according to "NICOTINE: HARDER TO KICK...THAN HEROIN" dated March 29, 1987 in the New York Times it is a monster to stop. But, my choice is to move away from smoke or not allowing it in my residence. Yet, I cannot judge anyone because I am a delivered former smoker. If anything I will empathize with the person. The same can be true for citizenship in the Kingdom of God. As a man not understanding the citizenship of the Kingdom, I blindly floated from one place to another, one relationship to another, one substance to another. And, the list of vagabond floating goes on and on. But, there must be a time in our quest for manhood and identity when we question if in fact we really understand. As with many grasped beliefs and personal doctrines some will fight to the last breath to hold onto their sacred cow and practices!

Church attendance does not guarantee you citizenship in the Kingdom of God. If we think we have done God a favor by going to a gathering of like-minded people, we truly err. Only be denouncing one kingdom can you then apply for citizenship in the next. This is normally the same thing for citizenship in other countries. Rarely can you be citizens of more than one country simultaneously. This is the same with God. Either you are a citizen of His kingdom, or you are a citizen of the kingdom of darkness. Dusk to dawn does not replace light and dark.

Reflection

Have you been on the receiving end of bad treatment because of your convictions concerning the Kingdom of God?

Have you rendered a prideful and unrighteous judgment on someone because of your view on their situation?

Can you in a basic way defend some aspects of the Kingdom of God; basic apologetic reasoning? Or are you prone to just parroting religious clichés with no foundation?

No Moldy Bread

We as men want to be in the forefront of the family and community, and we should! But, being in the forefront, in charge, or whatever we label it as comes with a price. Many look to us for answers. And, the worst thing we can do is pretend like we have them all. I learned very early in life that it was okay and even admirable to not have all the answers. However, cultural mores and cockiness has given us this *perceived* ability to be omniscient. It does not work.

Did we believe stupid stuff or what?

This is the same in our spiritual walk as well. We do not have all the answers. Once I came to Christ I was told by some well-meaning but very ignorant clergy that now all I had to do was to look to "da lawd" and He would give me all the answers I needed. They told me that I didn't need to ask anybody anything because God would reveal it all to me. Well, that lasted two weeks until I was stationed on a tropical island full of radiation and discovered what sunburn was. Oh yeah. They also told me that Black people didn't suffer from sunburn. Well, the only logic that I could possibly extract from my mind to justify their statement being truth was that I was pecan-tan and therefore vulnerable to the kryptonite of sun rays. Other than that there was no explanation of the peeling like a molting lizard. Wow! Did we believe stupid stuff or what?

We hold onto that moldy bread and then try to scrape off the mold and feed it to others.

There are keys in the Bible that tell us what we are to do in order to receive our daily bread. The problem has been and does continually presenting itself as us not wanting to replace moldy bread. The Hebrew people were able to gather manna for a prescribed timeframe of use. We are told as New Testament believers that we are to ask for daily bread. Then since this is so, why is it that we want the same bread that we have been carrying around since we first learned of sex in an alley with someone who told you that kissing three times would give you cooties at best or get a girl pregnant? We hold onto that moldy bread and then try to scrape off the mold and feed it to others. The same is true of our faith and Christian foundation.

We cannot lead without being led.

I don't know of anyone that walks this earth who has had a full revelation of God, the Word and needs no new revelation. Yet, we treat our people that look up to us subconsciously as morons because we subconsciously think we know it all. God tells us specifically that He only answers His own word. So, with all of our logic we should deduct that He will only answer His word or what He has told us to say! Correct? Then it is up to us to draw that from Him to us that we may pray it back to Him. This is in supposition that one does pray apart from a rote recitation over a meal when others are looking or something more than asking God for what we want.

We cannot lead without being led. Therefore, it is incumbent upon us to receive our instruction and direction daily; our daily bread. Then and only then can we say how much we are dependent upon God and interdependent on one another. Until then, at best we can produce is moldy bread that could make others sick. Now, don't get me wrong. I grew up cutting the mold off of bread in order to make a meal. It was required at times. And, there may be times when you may have to "initially" eat that moldy bready until another meal comes. You may be temporarily poor. But, you are not poor in God permanently! This is a bastion of ignorance that is often one of the extremes perpetuated in mainstream religion. Get that straight. And, the only excuses that you have for serving moldy bread once you know Who the Baker is and how to contact Him is that you are rebellious and prideful, wanting to be a legend in your own mind to others. Sadly, your pride will kill many. So, my brothers please at all costs stop serving your moldy bread. Go to God in supplications (asking Him what is on His heart for you to pray). Then pray that back to Him in order for Him to dispatch everything needed for good success for you and those who you are responsible for.

Reflection

How many things did you believe and then later found out after Biblical research and meditation were untrue?

How many times did you attempt to force these erroneous beliefs on others because this was all you allowed to come into your mind?

How many times have you blasted a fellow Christian because they challenged your religious sacred cows by attacking their salvation, life, or their church? **(A BIG ONE TO ANSWER)**

Competition of Competition

Men are warriors by nature. Yet, our nature of war tends to manifest in competition against one another. While at one time it was necessary for the competition in order to conquer and secure valuable real estate and resources and even brides, we have not taken it in the order needed. Now, there appears to be competition between one another. Meekness is taken as weakness. Yet, meekness is strength under control.

The sad part is even after this foundational revelation is given we still can reject the truth and attempt to embrace facts dictated by men.

Our strengths are given by God. We obtain no strength in our own right. So, with that being said arguments may arise about how we can increase our physical strength. Yet, in all reality we cannot do anything without the ability to breathe and the oxygen that is supplied by God! So, we cannot obtain anything without the foundation of God. How long have we erroneously thought it was us that had this ability to forge all of the strength needed? The sad part is even after this foundational revelation is given we still can reject the truth and attempt to embrace facts dictated by men. Facts change with rapid succession. However, Truth in the form of Jesus the Christ never changes. And, the Truth is that He is Truth; timeless and above even eternity.

While we are without God we compete with one another in order to place ourselves above one another. This is understandable because it is the way of humanity without Christ. Yet, when we embrace Christ as Savior we often will not allow Him to be Lord because we still wish to compete against one another. There should come a point in our lives where we have nothing to prove to anyone: even the devil. The best example that is given to us is the Lord Jesus. He never competed with the religious figures. Even though He was the embodiment of God on earth, He never competed to "show them who the boss was". Instead, He left the synagogue to teach among the people. He could have continued to strive in the synagogue, yet He didn't. But, there are far too many instances where men of God strive in the house of God; determined to prove how right or anointed their mindset is. This is in error. The times of Jesus in the synagogue most memorable were when He read from the Torah and was seated and when He scourged those who were defacing and defaming the house of God attempting to make it a den of thieves.

There should come a point in our lives where we have nothing to prove to anyone: even the devil.

So, the question that I am posing is why are there such competitive spirits in the Body of Christ that wish to rise to acclaim through titles and practice a form of spiritual penis envy? We are all in need of salvation because of sin. No one sin trumps another. The biggest sin is rejection of Christ's sacrifice. Yet, as we pass through Him we tend to bring such competitive spirits with us to the point of needing to be above one another. This is ludicrous because we all came from the same origin on earth; dirt! Again, our example being Christ Who never considered it robbery to even come to earth.

In the Body of Christ we are given different gifts. Our gifts and abilities are given for the express purpose of glorifying God. This is a very simple concept. However, we do not use them in that manner when we want to stack up our gift against another. I remember an old deacon that was very wise. He could store so many things in a small church until you wondered where he put those things! Then after a church meeting someone questioned if he was actually doing his job. They hinted that they could do a better job even though their gifting wasn't the same. I wasn't sure what this person's gift was other than to be abrasive to anyone that worshipped God.

The deacon looked at the leadership and told them that he did his job with excellence so they could lead the church.

After the competitive spirit manifested fully, the elderly deacon retreated and gave them the keys. Within a week there was to be a banquet in the church. The competitive brother found the chairs, but could not store them in the same efficient manner. As a matter of fact he even had to rent some chairs because he was sure that there were chairs missing in the church. Later, he discovered that they were right under his nose; neatly arranged with a table cloth over them. Then the dilemma of the lawn mower rose while the weeds looked like they were ready for a national tare convention. Then the other things began to pop up of which the competitive brother could not handle. Finally, he acquiesced to the elderly deacon but not with any apology. So, there was still a competitive spirit of "the next time" that was present. The deacon looked at the leadership and told them that he did his job with excellence so they could lead the church. Never did he get any apology. Yet, he served that church for so many years; more than anyone else if I am not mistaken. Sadly, this is present in many churches. One will look at the gifting and anointing of another with disdain, inferiority and even jealousy coupled with cockiness. One will try to outdo another in the form of "deepness" in the revelation of the Bible. Sometimes it sickens me to watch. Yet, I cannot place myself above it because most if not all men go through this stage in one form or another. Yet, some become stagnant in this area. I witness it often when dispatched to various churches; brothers that feel they have to compete for grandiose notice.

The difference is that in an organization, you can change the CEO to become the janitor while allowing the janitor to become a manager.

I liken the local body and congregation to the gates of Jerusalem. There are ten gates each with a distinctive purpose. Each gate never competed with the others in function. There were all attached to the same city, had a distinct function and also coexisted. Never did one gate argue or belittle another. If we use worldly wisdom we would say that one may be valued above another. But, each had its own purpose and was valued. One gate is often ignored when looking at Jerusalem; the Dung Gate. Now, what if that gate closed and would not be used because it wanted to be the Water Gate or the Horse Gate? How much disease and toxic materials would remain in Jerusalem? This is what was done when a city was laid under siege. While nothing could go in, what is often overlooked is that nothing, especially the dung, could be taken out!

In an organism such as the human body, if you do not allow the eye to see, it will never become a gall bladder.

The Body of Christ of which we are a part operates as an organism instead of an organization. So you ask, what is the difference? The difference is that in an organization, you can change the CEO to become the janitor while allowing the janitor to become a manager. In an organism such as the human body, if you do not allow the eye to see, it will never become a gall bladder. It is a very simple example that God shows us concerning the Body of Christ.

If we place this same principle on the body, we will see that if the anus would not function, the complete body would die from sepsis. So, what we deem as not desirable may very often be of great importance. When we jump into competiveness we remove ourselves primarily from the function and anointing God has for us for His glory and think we will move to where we think we are doing the best service. In other words our competitive spirit has just insinuated to God that He does not know best. Therefore, we begin to shape our own world not realizing that we have no world to be shaped.

... We need to stop being so competitive until we begin to be filled with pride.

We as men need to celebrate one another's gifting and abilities knowing that we all are given them to bring God glory. I celebrate the brother than can repair an automobile! I once tried to change my oil by myself to save $50. I ended up costing me over $300 for the damage I inflicted on my car! Why? Because I distinctly remember looking at the mechanic that I was going to use and telling him if I had to pay for my own oil then I may as well do it myself. When all the damage was done in prideful arrogance and insisted ignorance, the towing bill and repair bills along with the oil needed amounted to much more. Needless to say I did not take the car to the same mechanic that I was so arrogant with. I cowered and took it to another one. My point being, we need to stop being so competitive until we begin to be filled with pride. While healthy competition is needed, all competition is not healthy. The only competition that I may even consider would be who can serve one another at the lowest and least visible capacity. And, the other possibility would be who can say the he (or she if any women are reading) has been forgiven more by God. In the Body of Christ there is to be no competition at all. We are all doomed without accepting Christ and forgiven by the same measure in Him. Selah.

Reflection

When have you received a correction concerning a foundational truth and rejected it to continue grasping on the traditions of men?

Do you still find a need to have to prove something to someone in order to validate your calling or worth? Can your actions of preparation, performance and result be your only proof required?

Do you understand the difference between a Christian organization and an organism as related to the Body of Christ?

Floating Words

Words create worlds. Ask God. He spoke and everything came forth. Ironically, there are times when I will review the words spoken to me from God and also through others inspired by Him. These words can be through prayer in the Holy Spirit, from the inner whisper during worship, from others that allow themselves to be used of Him to speak who have an intimate relationship with Him and also by reading His love letters to us; the Bible. Either way, our words create things. We as men should now be very aware that our words are the creative force behind our existence. What we speak will create, fertilize or change the seed of a word prior. If it is a word from God such as His promises to us, our words either reinforce and hasten those promises or negate them because we kill the promise by negative and contrary words.

There is a communication between the Trinity that has no need to be audible or expressed because they are One yet Three.

One Sunday morning, as we were preparing to enter worship when Pastor Margo Wallace spoke that all words come from God. My spirit leaped. It was a moment in which you had to "catch" the rhema of God, not be taught the logos. I caught the rhema. It was in such a manner that I meditated on it all that day. All words truly come from God. Anything outside of God needs words! There is a communication between the Trinity that has no need to be audible or expressed because they are One yet Three. But, every other direction, command, creation or instruction must be from a word coming from God. The transmission is clear and concise. The reception or relay is where mankind had problems. The enemy has always taken God's word and distorted it. Lucifer took the words that God gave him and twisted them. He was to use those "words" to worship God. Instead he added things to it and twisted them. Another example is Adam. Yes, Adam twisted the instruction to Eve which cause her to (using a youthful metaphor) to get "caught up in her feelings" and listen to the serpent. A perfect example is when the serpent used twisted words in the Garden of Eden. He used a partially arranged collection of specific words to feed the hidden desires already in man thereby obtaining the earth. He uses misused words to get man to follow and worship him. He will use partial Scripture to cause division in the Body of Christ. And, even worse, he will plant partial Scripture in man to be passed on to families, community and even churches for generations at a time until someone somewhere picks up a Bible. Therefore, we must return to the foundational source of all words; God.

God told us that we will be snared by the words of our mouth. So, in essence we can be freed by the same process. Once Pastor Margo spoke that into the atmosphere and I had already been hearing to write concerning words, the connection was made. Far too often we have too many words. We speak religious clichés which in essence will be the same as a "waste your time curse". They have no foundation often in what God has ordained us to speak. We repeat the religious buzz words of the culture while immersing them with supposed Christian doctrine. These same words may have an ounce of truth hidden in a pound of lies. But, they "sound" good. These good sounding words find reception in us because we are not tuned into the Master Transmission of God. Therefore, we receive static that is louder than the transmission.

Men, we have to watch what we create.

Whenever a "word" is given we must immediately go back to the One that is the foundation and Originator of all words and His record of them: The Bible. This is how we judge words. That spoken word has already been released into the atmosphere and looking for a landing zone. When we inadvertently open our mouth to release any word into the atmosphere it takes on a life with no foreseen end. Men, we have to watch what we create. We can use the cliché of shaping our world with our words. But, the words begin somewhere to begin shaping which will end up being your world. I submit to you that your words still begin with God, within Him. But, the transmission of them rearranges them according to your communication coordinator which may be the enemy unless you have checks and balances in place; prayer, praise, worship, Bible study, pastor of grounded churches and accountability for our mouths from other people!

Reflection

Do you attach a location or target to the words you release?

What have you created or killed with your words?

Can you KYMS (Keep Your Mouth Shut)?

Once Upon A Time Called Now

Oh, I'll get it later. I'm going to make time for it. I think I can fit it in. Time is money. It's not time yet. These are all the phrases that we have used upon occasion. However, we are made in the image of God and after His likeness. When did He ever say, I'll get to you later. Your prayers are important to Him. Your needs are important to Him. Therefore there is no time like the present in God's eyes.

Men will make time. It's just that simple. God made time. Yet man will only make time if he is into his own world or if there is a benefit to the interruption. News flash! While this is our world for dominion it still belongs to God. Therefore, we are on His time not ours. And, it stands that while we think we are saving time, it is all His anyway. So, in essence we are only either living for Him as intended with the time allotted, or we are taking what He has given us for personal use and very possibly misuse.

... We cannot truly define time. So, we attempt by using the word "eternal".

Take for instance the phrase so often uttered "time is money". How can an eternal concept as time be measured by earthly understanding and value? Surely, we can say that we can define time. Yet, I ask what "time" does God operate in? We can get theologically deep and speak of *kairos* which is the Greek word for the opportune time of God or *chronos* which is our measurement of time on the earth. However, we cannot truly define time. So, we attempt by using the word "eternal". Yet, eternal is still an expression of time that we can understand even in not understanding the fullness of understanding time and its measurement. So, again, we define "time" in our own limited and humanly developed and articulated manufactured understanding. This can puzzle anyone attempting to grasp hold of something that is not attainable especially if we throw this mind cramp onto someone coming to God as if they need to pass this "test" in order for salvation to take full effect. Can I submit to you that before there was time, salvation was in order? As normal, I won't give you a straight line to the prize. I'll just point that it's over yonder in the Book of Revelation between chapter twelve and the end.

I have been accused of thinking too much when it comes to God and His word. I confess! I do! I want to know everything about Him; how He thinks as much as HUMANLY possible, what He sees in me as an individual, and even how He wishes me to handle His time! If you want me to get depressed and be filled with awe simultaneously, let me meditate on everything I have done that was contrary to God's will for me and how He yet waited for me to still love me! I will bawl like a smacked baby!

... I am realizing that I am wasting time trying to define it.

Well, it is my muse that we cannot describe anything concerning a measurement of time. Therefore, we should seek Him for every waking moment's use. I won't get many that agree, but we cannot even measure correctly time. And this even includes eternity. Why? Eternity is actually a measurement of time, or at least an attempt to describe the ability to not be able to measure it. So, if we are to measure time or the inability to measure it and call it eternity, is that not still a way to measure with an attempt to measure time? Again, this is my muse. So, since God's ways and thoughts are above our ways and thoughts, then it would be logically illogical to say that we understand time. No. We do not understand time. We understand at the most, eternity. And, since that is the most that we understand, then it would be an assumption (by me at least) that God operates and dwells outside of eternity. So, while we think we can communicate effectively the measurement of time, I am realizing that I am wasting time trying to define it. I stopped trying when I read Isaiah 66:1. Ah, I slipped and gave you a location. Well, since heaven is God's throne and earth is His "footstool", then where is His "head"? I now will be silent because it is in a place that cannot explain. He exists in a place that can't be described.

God saved us "time" before we even entered into this realm!

Now why would I take up precious time to say all of this? I say this because when a man says that he will do something later he is actually saying that he understands and controls time, especially when it is dealing with his spouse and family. While we are made in the image of God, we don't understand all that there is to know about Him. So, we have no time to take our time. Am I saying to run or rush to do everything and anything? Not in the least. I am saying that if we grasp a nugget given to us concerning time written in Revelation 13:8 then we can understand that before we could touch time, God already saved us and gave us "time". The Lamb was slain before the foundation of the world. (I gave another location away. Stay tuned in the reading for other clues) Then as I love to dig deeper for understanding (English is such a bastardized and daily expanding language) I see in the Greek that the word "foundation" actually means the "disruption" of the world. God saved us "time" before we even entered into this realm!

God was not mad when He said "Adam where are you".

Therefore my brethren, value the gift that we cannot describe. The gift of time was given to us before there was even time. How? Because God gave us life before we could even grasp the concept of death thereby saving us time and allowing us to practice out eternal living before time actually began. The next time Genesis is read in your hearing, think of it as this. God was not mad when He said "Adam where are you". He just wanted to show him that He had already saved him "time". All Adam and Eve had to do was flow in what God had set before them; an end of time which had already begun to end and to return to Him as He dwelt outside of "time". He in essence was telling us, "Once upon a time called NOW, the Lamb was slain". Never "get around to it". Be about doing "it" without attempting to control what you can't explain. Selah.

Reflection

Do you value time as your most valuable and priceless commodity?

Do you realize that time is not your friend?

Can you understand that God does not operate in any expression of time or inability to fully express time such as eternity? Do you agree or disagree?

Return to Hebraic Christianity

While the subtitle of this may be threating to some, it actually isn't. For those that love simplicity, this is the most soothing direction that one can take concerning Christianity. I choose purposely not to get into arguments or even gentle debates concerning many aspects of Christianity. While denominations are the norm in this era, our collective foundations for everything Christian is Hebraic. Am I saying that we are all to practice Judaism? No. What I am saying is that we as men should have more of a grasp on the history of our faith which would give us more of an understanding to pass it on to subsequent generations. We tend to have history on other avenues of our existence but not the history concerning our faith. Could this be the main contributor in the often impotent belief that we have? I would say so.

While denominations are the norm in this era, our collective foundations for everything Christian is Hebraic.

Our mindset concerning faith and Christianity somehow attempts to ignore the foundational truths of the Old Testament. We have started at the cross with no understanding that the prophets and Law prior were both fulfilled in Christ before He was crucified, buried and risen. Unfortunately we have become so churched that we think this was the Genesis of our denomination. We are truly wrong. Why would I say this? I say this because in our desire to be good Christians embracing the "present culture" we can have a Christian mindset that is in no way Biblical. I say this because many arguments have risen and caused strife concerning such small issues or in times past justification for things totally wrong. For instance, at one time the Bible was incorrectly referred to as a justification for slavery. The culture of that day allowed "good Christians" to enslave another person and consider them less than human. However, there were areas that were overlooked that would have debunked the Christian mindset of the day as un-Biblical while indeed there were records of slavery in the Scriptures.

All that the Torah spoke of pointed to Christ.

But, if we return to our Hebraic foundations of Christianity, we can see that all that the prophets wrote pointed to Christ. All that the Torah spoke of pointed to Christ. And, as in the Biblical account in Luke 9:28-36 and Matthew 17:1-13 describes the Transfiguration. Both of these were drawn up into Christ since He is the fulfillment of all. Yet, Jewish existence never ended at that point.

Reflection

Can you give basic foundational truths for our Christian faith and the relation to the Hebrew feasts?

Are you confined to denomination and possibly restricted beliefs concerning Christianity?

Would you take needed time to discover the beauty of Hebrew connections to your current doctrinal truths?

I Know All About That!

I simply cringe when I hear the above titled phrase come out of a man's mouth! What that says to me is that I know it all and no one can tell me anything about what I don't want to know about. But, in reality, we only know what we know. We don't know what we don't know unless we allow someone to show us that we don't know "all" about nothing! This has been the prideful presentation of a warped manhood of self-enlightenment and awareness.

All I could hear his friend say was, "I already know about that; I know all about that."

I once took my son and his best friend fishing. While I knew the uncle of the friend and his love of the pastime of fishing (we often fished together) I wasn't completely sure that he had imparted this into his nephew. Nevertheless, I took him anyway. My son and I had enjoyed the time as I had taught him how to properly and surgically cast after many attempts and him hooking me in the back of my neck and other painful locations on my body! Well, the young angler now was attempting to teach what he had been taught; a trait that I instilled in him. All I could hear his friend say was, "I already know about that; I know all about that." After two or three interruptions from my peacefulness and tranquility, I laid my rod on the grass and walked over. This little arrogant being told me that his uncle was a fisherman "therefore" he knew all about how to do it. My son tried to warn him. He told him that he needed to learn and not know everything. I was surprised at the rebuke this child was giving someone. In his own juvenile way he was telling him to listen and shut his mouth; which he didn't heed. He even told him the consequence; me taking them home if it was not to be a peaceful and fun outing. In times like these I normally mixed fun and pleasure with impartation. My son had grown to expect and like it. He was a little irate at his friend for destroying his time with me as he would have questions answered and receive nuggets that he could ponder on during the week.

We don't know what we don't know unless we allow someone to show us that we don't know "all" about nothing!

I gave him a challenge. If he could effectively cast the line in the middle of the pond, and it didn't even have to be far out, I would leave him alone to his professed wisdom and innate ability. He agreed. After the first five or six times with the line going nowhere, it became a tangled mess. I let him continue just informing him that he had to untangle his own line. I had fish to catch. After a frustrating two more casts, he hooked his own finger and started bawling like a baby; this big strapping boy! You would have though the child was shot in a war zone firefight! It didn't help when I laughed at him not to ridicule him but to get his attention. Yet, when he finally acknowledged that he didn't know it all, and that a relative or friends expertise is not yours he wanted to leave. But, I made them stay there with me. Eventually, he was actually casting and even caught a few fish. But, what he realized was that he didn't like fishing. He just liked knowing someone who did and fitting into the surroundings. He never wanted to go fishing again opting out for TV viewing and video games.

We were not born knowing anything or everything.

This is a lesson for men. We only know what we been taught. And, we know nothing other than being taught. So, whatever you have been taught has an impact upon the way you think, operate and grow. We hide behind achievements and possessions. Yet, if you strip away all of the achievements, possessions and titles, we are all that little boy; knowing in an immature way everything! We were not born knowing anything or everything. From the time we were birthed, we had to be laid on our mother's breast and learn how to suck. The problem is when we were to be growing and exploring, we may have been sucking. So, in this situation we made all of our spiritual, intellectual and spiritual growth centered upon a nipple instead of progressing to teeth.

It is not what we achieve. It is what we overcome.

Now, in manhood our first objective should be is to be real. Real men will readily admit that they do not know everything. We need to get rid of the façade of accomplishments and replace it with the humility and gratefulness of what God has done for and in us. It is not what we achieve. It is what we overcome. I have met the most accomplished men in the world that had the fortitude of a dead earthworm because in their achievements they found skeletal vertical stamina in order to stand tall. Take away the achievements and they were shells of men. In this day of transferring riches if your realness is based on monetary currency, you may be real in shifts just like the financial markets of the world!

"Lord, let me continue to learn that I may become more ignorant."

Upon entering seminary, in my very first class, Systematic Theology (boy was I asking for it), I penned something on my notebook. While I am not a proponent of saying that seminary gives or increases anointing, I do say that some need to go for their own development. You do not go to seminary to be called. You go to seminary to learn. You really don't need to go if you are called. (At this point I just upset most of the denominational clergy of the world.) Perhaps a personal contact will allow us to reason together at another time. But, in this graduate setting, I remember penning on my note book, "Lord, let me continue to learn that I may become more ignorant." I have always kept this humility of learning no matter how "different" I think the source is. Yet, with our manhood we wish to pick and choose who we learn from. I gave the example in a previous work about learning from a wino (person who lives, breaths, drinks and functions for drunkenness from cheap wine). While his appearance was not the best, if you would listen to him amazement would fall. He was discovered later as having much more on the ball than his detractors.

So, my brothers, I say this. We do not know it all. And, if you know it all think of Adam. He knew more than God knew according to the legend forming in his own mind. This is why he gave Eve faulty information facilitating her biting the fruit and consummating him following suit to the demise of humanity. I will use some hard language here. If you don't like it, go see if you can get a refund for the book or just give it to another man. But, if you cannot take correction or at least allow someone to show you another view that may have not been within your historical paradigm, you are an immature and fearful boy at best and a fool at worst. Even a servant could correct his master and with no reward. How many servants, boys, WOMEN, clergy, etc. have come to you, yet you don't esteem the message because of the delivery method? Get right, or get left my brothers. Just because it comes in Satan's limousine does not mean it's not God's blessing. I pray to hear a marked decrease in the all-consuming men's rock of hiding; "I know all about that". Selah.

Reflection

Can you receive correction from a source that you personally do not esteem?

Are you weak in that you can only receive correction from another man?

Can you take correction from a person that is not operating in a title or position as long as it is true? Can you even recognize the truth in a correction?

What You Hear, You Live

I experienced something very interesting while going through a very difficult time of my life. I was in a program to treat the effects of post-traumatic stress disorder and learned quite a bit about the subconscious. It amazed me on a spiritual level because of how God created our brain to operate. I had read studies on subliminal suggestions and how they work. So, leave it to me to find spiritual connections to what science is trying to say. And, now since this was needed, I applied it spiritually which helped accelerate my treatment.

Music of itself is amoral.

Instead of listening to rain at night which is what the program provided, I would play at a low level sermons or worship music. I noticed when I awoke there was a marked difference in my sleep and waking. I also did the same along drives or commutes. I would play anything such as audio notes for examinations, sermons, lectures or anything I wanted "imbedded" into me. And, when it was time for recall, I had it. So, I guess what I am saying to my brothers is that you are what you listen to.

What lyrics do you allow to permeate your spirit?

Music of itself is amoral. What you do with it is what makes it moral or immoral. Again, Lucifer never lost his ability to make music, nor did God remove music from creation or heaven. There is continually worship and music in heaven. So, while music hasn't change in its core existence, the purpose of it has been tampered with. So, my brothers, there is a limit on what you listen to. What lyrics do you allow to permeate your spirit? What thoughts accompany those lyrics that are not wholesome? And, can you change the message of the music that you hear? These are all things that need to be addressed when we allow our ears to become gates to our spirits. Music is a universal language that never needed to be taught or interpreted. Music does not need permission to enter your spirit. Think of your elementary school days. Whenever you were tasked to learn something new and commit it to memory, music was the vehicle. Why would the enemy look for something new? Psalms were music. And they were powerful in their worship retention. So, we know that music must be monitored. God didn't remove music from creation because the original purpose for it is to worship Him.

Both good and bad sounds are in the atmosphere.

The next part is what you hear as far as the Word of God. Too often men will attend worship service on Sunday, yet forget that every day we are to worship. Could it be that those drives can be avenues of meditation? Instead of the sports channel or the latest music playlist, why not pop in the impartation from Sunday? I guarantee you as one who has proven this statement; you will find something new each time you listen to that same sermon. I have turned into somewhat of a hoarder when it comes to sermons. Those words that have been preached to me through lineage, I have embraced. There are times when I will go very far back and listen to something that was ministered many years ago and still get some extra mileage from it. This is needed in order for a continued and sustained growth. God's word is timeless. Just as sermons from Charles Spurgeon and other spiritual generals are still used today, your pastor's sermons are used continually.

Even in our social circles we must guard our ears. If we partake of drama and gossip, it will seep into our very souls. If we are in the middle of many complainers or detractors of forward progress, we begin to act like that as well. All of these things need to be considered. Knowing that your words have power and life, why would you not think that other words also carry this power? Both good and bad sounds are in the atmosphere.

The speech that you utter goes into your spirit first. It leaves your vocal chords and enters into your inner ear before even leaving your mouth. Therefore it sinks into your spirit before it even leaves your body. So, when you utter the word of God, it enters into your spirit before being released into the atmosphere. Therefore, we live what we hear. Jesus said His words were spirit and life. Selah.

Reflection

What do you keep in your ear gate (ear) where faith comes to first?

How do you view music?

Can you discern between the sounds in the universe?

My Daddy the Prophet

As we position ourselves to be the head of the household in which we are placed, we are to be the prophet as well. All of the hoopla about a prophet has been tainted in the New Testament believers especially those of the Western culture. Yet, we still have the responsibility of the performance of the one who prophetically leads!

Women are forced to step up into a position of leader either by default or be deception.

A prophet is a person who speaks for God and an inspired person or leader. In the case of the New Testament prophet, he is one who points that way to our Savior, Jesus the Christ while instructing, rebuking and correcting according to the Word of God. There is no spookiness about the function and responsibility. By pointing those that we father toward the Lord, we are fulfilling our mandate as the priest, prophet and even protector. Why would I say protector as well? I say this because as we live in front of them, they also begin to walk as we walk; in faith. Therefore, they embrace the One that protects us and thereby they are protected.

God spoke to both the man and woman in Genesis and told both to have dominion.

In too many instances society removes the responsibility of the man from the position of prophet and distorts the function. Women are forced to step up into a position of leader either by default or be deception. In no way am I saying that a woman is not capable of leader according to creation. In fact what I am saying is that when we do not stand in the position, she is well capable of being a leader. God spoke to both the man and woman in Genesis and told both to have dominion. It was never a question about the power and ability of the woman, only her position and the order according to God on earth. And, to continually place the truth in plain sight, she is only to submit to those in authority on earth as ordained by God, and to her own husband (the man to whom she is married), as unto the Lord. Never is a woman a weaker vessel unless you are only viewing her in a physical sense. Even if this is your view try carrying and bearing a child.

They see this huge person of wisdom that knows the answer to everything...
Therefore, when our children look to us as daddy, they see the person that is to point the direction for them. They see this huge person of wisdom that knows the answer to everything; what they should do, how they are to accomplish something and where we are going. They do not see just a person. They see the prophet; the one who is hearing from God, endowed with all wisdom from out of this world and pointing the way that we should go. They see Daddy, the Prophet!

Reflection

Do you accept that man and woman both were given dominion in the earth?

What prophetic guidance are you giving those assigned to your care?

Can you prophetically and continually point someone to Christ?

Fears

Our insecurity in manhood stems from the examples and expectations that people have placed on us and portrayed to us. As stated earlier, our examples may not have been the greatest. Even in instances where there were true examples, none have come close to who God is as Father. Regardless of how pristine our example has been, nothing will come close to the example of God as Father.

Often we learn by trial and error. Our insecurities of relationships specifically marriage hinder us from admitting that we need a higher authority. Men, by societal permission, are encouraged to try out many different relationships in hope of finding what we think we need. This is not very wise. Often we think that something better can be at the next turn. We forget that perfection has not rested in us. Therefore, it is a false expectation for someone else to be perfect for us. If we are careless, we spend the majority of our lives looking for that perfect woman when we ourselves are imperfect. This is possibly why men feel comfortable going from relationship to relationship in modern times besides the fact that society gives them this as an expectation.

Is dating wrong? Not by any means.

In the past, when a man found a woman who he wanted to wed, he dealt directly with her; forsaking all others. Somehow in this society, we moved away from courting and embraced dating. Is dating wrong? Not by any means. However, when that person is identified as one who he wishes to spend his life with in the covenant of marriage, all dating should be turned to courting; learning of her ways, fears, desires and goals. I question at what point does a man realize that this woman is the proverbial one? Does he recognize it after two dates, four, or one hundred thirty nine? When?

Often in present society, dating gives us options of moving out of the way if there is something that we don't like. This view even continues in many marriages. No more is the covenant of marriage sacred as it was intended. Marriage has taken a move from God's covenant and reflective relationship to one of contract and convenience.

Our understanding has shifted from covenant to contract. If we maintain the covenant, we will hold marriage dear as it was intended. Once we revert to marriage as being a contract, then it can be dissolved with any difficulty arising. God never intended marriage to be broken. Nor did He ever say that we are to marry on a trial basis. We cheapen His beauty and purpose when we view this as society does.

Fears of judgment arise in our relationships of exposure. While men are expected to be hard soldiers, we are actually fragile in differing ways from the woman. We don't seem to express our feelings as quickly as women. And, often when we do express them, by hiding them for so long, they come out in a harsh manner; even anger. Our feelings are just as deep as a woman; maybe even more so. Where women are more emotional, we share a fear of showing emotion.

As a boy, we are told not to cry.

I find it very interesting, yet disheartening, how even in the church we can display such strength and poise in the midst of personal turmoil. Where a woman can tell someone what she is feeling or express those emotions quickly, we deny they even exist. Could this be the reason that our life expectancy is shorter? Where a woman will all those penned up feelings to come out, relieving her of the stress, a man will continue as if nothing is bothering him. The next mutual and emotional thing you know we are in some form of physical distress because of stress. Is it a hard thing to express emotions? It is definitely not at all hard to express emotions. But, until we root back to the beginning of this problem, we will never advance beyond our conditioning.

As a boy, we are told not to cry. We are told that we are becoming men and grown men don't cry. Well, in the example of Jesus Christ, the epitome of Man, we see that weeping or crying with displays of emotion is not feminine. Although there may be a difference in expression of the same emotions between genders, there needs to be healthy expression nonetheless.

Our relationships begin with a relationship with Him.

Our fears often reflect our inadequacies whether real or perceived. We are told not to be weak. But, in reality, we are weak in some area of our lives. This is where God fills us. He tells us in 2 Corinthians 12:9 *"My grace is sufficient for you, for My strength is made perfect in weakness."* Therefore most gladly I will rather boast in my infirmities, that the power of Christ may rest upon me." It is hard for us if we don't understand that the power of God rests in our acknowledgement of Him, desire for Him to guide us, and our permission for Him to mold us. At some point in our lives we must reach out to Him; tell Him that we need help in fulfilling His intended purpose in life. And, we definitely must admit to those who are close to us that we don't know everything that we should. This is a learning process for all parties involved. The joy in this is that God assists us in becoming men after His heart.

Our relationships begin with a relationship with Him. There is no other way to get around it. Regardless of whether the relationship is a man to man relationship, a plutonic relationship with a woman, or a romantic and committed relationship with a woman, there can be no true growth apart from

God. And I am very clear that a man-to-man relationship will never be one for romance or marriage in my eyes according to God.

Every relationship requires a degree of communication.

Our relationship with Him is premier. In the beginning, God created us that we may have that intimate relationship. He is a relational God. This is proven in the fact that He constantly reaches out to us to restore and maintain that which was formed from the beginning; even to the point of sacrificing His own Son in order for reconciliation to be accomplished.

Ironically, relationship with God is often confused with church attendance and religious observances. While this may be an aspect of communing with Him, it is not the catch-all relationship. Every relationship requires a degree of communication. In deeper relationships, such as we are to experience with God, intimacy is desired and required. This cannot be obtained in once a week worship services. The weekly worship service is a corporate gathering. We also have intimate and private encounters. It is in these settings that we are one on one with God, such as Adam had in the Garden. Adam was continually in the presence of the Creator with such a communion and intimacy to where he didn't even know that he needed a helper. It is at this point where we enter in a zone of total joy and intimacy.

There was a realization that God is the best companion that one could ever hope for.

I have experienced this in my own life. There was a time when confusion set in concerning companionship. I was pitifully desperate to find my Eve. However, in my efforts to do this, I was always trying to 'create' an Eve. God gives all of us the foundations and requirements for a godly woman. But, in our haste we often try to manufacture one according to our own desires; apart from His intentions. I would attempt to bring my 'creation' to God and tell Him that this was my 'Eve'. He would gently tell me no. In my stubbornness, I would again present her to Him. When God sees our stubborn attitudes, often we receive what it is that we think we want. It was only a matter of time before I would ask God to fix my mess; I had stumbled onto Legion instead of Eve. But, when I surrendered and understood that being alone is not the same as being lonely, I was truly blessed.

As I began to spend time in His presence, nothing else mattered. There was a realization that God is the best companion that one could ever hope for. I even became so oblivious to my past conditions that there was actually no strong desire to share my time with anyone else! Once I came to this point, only then He could bless me with a wife.

Marriage is the only relationship until death.

A couple of years ago, I received such a revelation and blessing from a man of God that I have treasured it and passed it on to others. Archbishop Wilbert McKinley of Elim International Fellowship in Brooklyn, New York, who has since transitioned to be with our Lord, gave me a flood of wisdom in less than thirty seconds. He told me that my live should be arranged in five tiers. First, God for He is the Source of all life. My relationship with Him is tantamount to survival and fulfillment. Second, would be myself as submitted to God ever seeking to be closer in intimacy to Him. I needed to have time to walk out or enact what I learn from the Father through the Holy Spirit. Only then will I continually grow. Next, when the time came, I would have my spouse. This is the person that God blessed me with. I would be entrusted to love and honor them; loving God through them. Marriage is the only relationship until death. Children leave home. Friends move away. The spouse is joined with you as one in the eyes of God. Next my family and children would be in order. This was to occur only after your spouse. The relationship with your children and extended family does not supersede that of your spouse. Since the marriage covenant reflects a heavenly principle, we must look to Him in order to fully understand and grow with it. Finally, there is your vocation, ministry and career or employment. He told me that if these things would be placed in order, God would be free to bless everything that I touched. I never forgot that day in 2004. I had tapped into something which no one had ever explained to me concerning the order of God for my daily.

In my mind this man surely was at least seven feet tall!

To this day, I remember that with such accuracy for many reasons. One reason was that I had been listening to many recordings of his teachings and sermons for years. In my mind this man surely was at least seven feet tall! But, when I met him, he was short in stature but began to grow in my sight as he imparted this to me. I left his presence with a perpetual Selah moment from that one minute impartation; forever to have that etched in my spirit.

So therefore, our fears are nothing but ignorance. They are fear of death, fear of people, fear of failure, and fear of rejection. And before someone attempts either to give me credit for being so spiritually deep (or label me as a plagiarist) Apostle Nate Holcomb describes all of this in his book "Life Beyond Fear". Let us get past the fear and the erroneous relationships that perpetuate constant fear of failure and rejection so we can flow in His intended function. Selah.

Reflection

Do you have a fear of the exposing of your inadequacies?

Do you have a fear of death, people, rejection or failure? Can you properly identify them?

Do you have a fear of communication? Why?

Prayer Life versus a Life of Prayer

I often wonder what caused us as men not to pray as we once did. In the Word of God as recorded in the New Testament, men were involved constantly in prayer and meditation. We were in the meetings, even leading them. Yet, modern man has somewhat fallen away from the discipline of prayer. It is time we returned.

The model for all men is Jesus. He was up early in the morning praying. While I won't attempt to set some sort of doctrine concerning the hour of prayer, I can say that personally the early morning hours (the fourth watch between 3 am and 6 am) for me is awesome in prayer and meditation. It is an hour that I have no descriptive words for concerning the peacefulness and receptive senses.

... *We need to know His will in order to become agents of change.*

I do realize that there are times when we keep schedules that are alternative schedules; those not conducive to a dawn to dusk operation. However, the point being presented is that Jesus began with prayer before His day, not after. We speak of God's will being done on earth as it is in heaven. Yet, we need to know His will in order to become agents of change. This is why it imperative that prayer is offered first for ourselves, then for our family, our community then for all men. We must pray. It is the life of a Christian.

The disciples noticed how Jesus was adamant about prayer in the morning. They would observe Him leaving to be alone. My thoughts as I read this concerned them following Him! This was the One that moved in such a way and they had left all for. Why not follow Him? I would want all I could from Him. But, perhaps this was a warning of things to come. Now, we must reverse this trend and return to the discipline that was modeled for us through Christ; prayer.

Let us as men be as pointed and targeted with our prayers as we are with our communications.

Another observation was that Jesus prayed targeted prayers. When He prayed prior to anything transpiring, He didn't pray for anything but that particular daily situation. He didn't pray for a healing and include prayers of provision. He prayed to the Father for specifics and then gave thanks for that petition. We often feel that we must pray long and arduous prayers in order to satisfy a religious requirement. This is nothing more than qualifying for Pharisaical exercises. It would be tantamount to praying a blessing over food and including the state of the world's ailments in a foreign country along with the upcoming church meeting. (I have been in the presence of such prayers and was almost unconscious before the meal.) No, let us learn to pray targeted prayers. Otherwise, we will pray amiss and loose the connection with those around us.

A person that will offer long and drawn out prayers for everything but the instructed petition possibly is under the microscope of their own guilt. This person may very well not have a prayer life in private. Therefore, when put "on the spot" in public they subconsciously overcompensate. Let us as men be as pointed and targeted with our prayers as we are with our communications. We can view John 17 as the longest recorded prayer of Christ and the prayer in the Garden of Gethsemane as the most intense prayer.

Not to shift blame, but we are often taught that He will give us the desires of our hearts.

In the next step, we should readily grasp inconvenient prayers. Our prayers should always, always be "not my will but Thine will be done". I have been so very guilty of not praying His will!!! Not to shift blame, but we are often taught that He will give us the desires of our hearts. Yes, He will! But, the desires He gives us of our heart are His desires in order to pray back to Him; not what we want!

The Father kept whispering, "No, My son".

I can recall praying for a specific situation because "I" wanted it to happen. The Father kept whispering, "No, My son". But, like a tantrum qualified brat I kept asking. Finally, He allowed me to receive what I had borderline demanded of Him. Forty months later (literally forty months, the time of testing) I was so badly wounded and fatigued from my demand that I wear a scar and got a testimony for so many others who demand that God give them what they want. While this may be one of the most memorable moments of total madness in my spiritual walk, it was not the only one. Thank God for His mercies being new every day!

Experiences such as these help us understand that the inconvenient prayers and submission to His will have safety as a byproduct of obedience. Often my well-being hinged on obedience in the natural as well as the spiritual submission to Him. I have heard in the spirit not to go a certain direction or accompany an individual. For the most part, I have always obeyed the unction to deviate. I cannot personally recall one time when it was not for my benefit.

In memories like these, I find my best examples of continuing with inconvenient prayers; Thy will be done.

Yet, there were times when I prayed, heard what to do and did contrary to what was pressed upon me. I paid for it in some manner. So, with the inconvenient prayer of His will being done, I would have been in a form of safety and provision other than what I experienced. Now, do not think for one moment that all things initially are so horrific. There were times that the deviance was so wonderful only to transform later into something that was horrible. Talk about flipping the script, this is a wonderful example of God's omniscient protection.

It was so very wonderful until before I knew it, I was drawn into a trap.

In memories like these, I find my best examples of continuing with inconvenient prayers; Thy will be done. Why? I remember these because initially everything appeared as if I had made the right decision. Surely God didn't speak loud enough. Or, even if He did, I must have had a choice in this and chose the right way. Not! I was dumber than a bag of hammers. It was so very wonderful until before I knew it, I was drawn into a trap. My desire to have my will accomplished over His will produced my results. And, therefore I was caught up in my results which were contrary to His will. It was never pretty! Thank God for His mercies!

The most painful transgressor against you is the one person you need to pray for with fervency.

Finally, my brothers, we are to pray unselfish prayers! I know you may have just turned the page, so I just may write it again so you won't miss this point. The most unselfish prayer to pray is for that one that wounded or transgressed against you. The most painful transgressor against you is the one person you need to pray for with fervency. About right now you should be twitching. You can recall more than one instance of pain. Yet, I can speak from experience of the liberating and transforming power of this principle.

... After forgiving you must pray for the transgressor!

The most painful wounds come from family, not enemies. Those close to you in familial relations inflict the worse wounds. No doubt they were also wounded in some manner. Therefore, it is an innate thought that they must get you back before you get them first. We have already spoken of forgiveness. But, I must reiterate with no relief the importance of forgiveness. And, after forgiving you must pray for the transgressor! There is no other way to survive. You must forgive them and then pray fervently for them until you are free! Notice I did not say that you were to walk in the rain with kicks and giggles stomping in puddles. There may be some things that you cannot experience with the person that caused pain. But, you must forgive them and elevate them to the Lord.

Your unselfish prayers avail much for that person.

God wishes us to understand the limitations of operation even though you may have forgiven the person. The limitations may be because of the person not you. Your unselfish prayers avail much for that person. And, as an added bonus of obedience, you begin to understand the person's spiritual place which will cause you to experience God's sorrow. You will even experience to a level how God felt toward us at one time. Then you will have a small smidgen of God's mind and heart. I cannot explain how this transformed my life! It still didn't change what happened to me. But, it did change how I viewed it. Whatever the relation of this person to you, it is the action that offended you. We do not wrestle with flesh and blood. Therefore, even though flesh and blood was what offended you in our eyes, it was only the vehicle of the spirit operating behind the offense. So, just as Christ unselfishly died in our place, we must unselfishly pray for this person to come to Him. Selah.

I drive speaking to Him or listening for His whisper.

So, what is the difference between a prayer life and a life of prayer? I submit to you that it is not the frequency of going to prayer, but the infrequency of not praying. I walk down the street literally speaking to God in my mind or even audibly. I drive speaking to Him or listening for His whisper. I realize that by putting this in print someone will think I am in need of medication or label me a fanatic. But, what is the difference of me doing this and another person concentrating on revenge? Only the application of life separates us. In am speaking to Life in order to give life, while the other person is thinking of taking life.

I want to always speak to Him and listen for Him speaking to me!

I try to speak to Him concerning everything, and I do mean everything. I even speak to Him constantly concerning my feelings, confusion, and confessing shortcomings. Yes, you do know your shortcomings are sin, right? And, He said to confess or agree with Him on it so He can be faithful and just. I do just that. So where a person may want to be considered pious and pray for a specific amount of time, I don't want to measure time unless it is time that I am "not" in communication with Him! I want to always speak to Him and listen for Him speaking to me!

You may walk or press into sin but never fall into it.

Is this fanatical? Very much so! And, I make no apologies for it considering I, as a man, have failed myself, family and community because of my ignorance or plain refusal to pray! The stakes are too high to play this game my brothers. We are to pray without ceasing. I find myself even waking in the middle of the night and speaking to Him. Never do I ever want to not speak to Him. An added value of this practice is that you will never "just do" what you know is wrong. You will never fall into sin. You may walk or press into sin but never fall into it. Ask Adam. Adam never just fell into the transgression. He chose and nurtured his desire to sin. So, there is a measure of safety and comfort in a life of prayer.

Therefore, we need to practice a life of prayer instead of just a prayer life. Why would I state this in such a way? I say it because I must die daily in Christ. So, with that being said as I live, move and have my being in Him, I also have a life of prayer just as He did. I am constantly connected to the Father just as Christ is. Selah.

Reflection

Do you communicate through prayer with God on a continual basis; just having conversations and listening to His guidance?

Do you practice prayer because it's on the calendar? And, is it relegated to rote (lifeless) repetition?

Do you limit your types of prayer? Do you understand the various types?

Family

The nuclear unit of creation by God is the family. While Adam, alone without the physical presence of Eve, was an individual, had no one with who to respond and could operate for a limited amount of time. God foresaw the need for companionship. Alas, Eve was released to be a help meet for him. Additionally, what we see concerning the first family is central to our understanding of manhood. Adam, the head, was responsible for Eve. This is a primary key. After the fall, God approached Adam first, not Eve. Even though he was not the initiator of the rebellion per se (or was he), he was responsible in God's eyes.

Man, created in His image, is the mirror in the physical realm of what God is to us in the spirit realm.

We as men are responsible for the family's well-being. Our initial responsibility is to God. Once we understand that God has given us the mandate to stand as head and not dictator then we will begin to seek Him and guide those in our care toward a relationship as well. Understanding that we are the symbolic source here on earth will quicken our understanding of God's position as Source.

Man, created in His image, is the mirror in the physical realm of what God is to us in the spirit realm. It is very interesting that we tend to be the source of all things only to prove our manhood. But, if we honestly look to Christ as our example, we understand the gravity of this position. Paul tells us in Ephesians 5:25-29 KJV:

> *Husbands, love your wives, just as Christ also loved the church and gave Himself for her, that He might sanctify and cleanse her with the washing of water by the word, that He might present her to Himself a glorious church, not having spot or wrinkle or any such thing, but that she should be holy and without blemish. So husbands ought to love their own wives as their own bodies; he who loves his wife loves himself. For no one ever hated his own flesh, but nourishes and cherishes it, just as the Lord does the church.*

This position as husband and head requires us to sacrificially die for the wife whom God has trusted us to love and guide. A heavy dose of responsibility for the beauty of the foundation of family is what we receive. Why is this? This is because our death will primarily be to our own desires and mindsets. We are to begin the death process in ourselves.

Perhaps when Adam knew that Eve would die because of the rebellion, he couldn't bear that she was alone and followed her.

In view of this and this is only my personal view is that Adam, too, died for his wife and her transgressions. We see that he did not partake first in what Eve did. However, he did follow her. I speak as not to form a doctrine, but just as provoking a thought. Perhaps when Adam knew that Eve would die because of the rebellion, he couldn't bear that she was alone and followed her. Again, this is just a thought to ponder. I say this to liken it to the actions of Christ. He died for us who were dead already because of sin and rebellion. At the point of Eve stepping into death, Adam had not yet received the penalty of rebellion. He was still very much eternal. As I look at this example, I am in awe that once a person has stepped into death and sin, how many times do we follow for whatever reasons? Please do not take this scenario as anything other than a pondering of why Adam continued on in the same vein that Eve chose.

The men of the family were the priests, providers and protectors.

Men were the premier examples in Biblical writings. The men of the family were the priests, providers and protectors. As a matter of fact, they were in such a priestly position, that their actions or inactions created the welfare of the family to be blessed or cursed! Thank God for the New Covenant where there is no difference male or female when it comes to the grace of our Lord Jesus Christ! Otherwise there would be many families that are cursed because of the actions of the man! The actions of men have blessed many a family. Their stand for righteousness strengthened and protected the other family members. Yes, the Bible was written in a patriarchal society. But, even in this vein, we still see the character of God portrayed. The woman may not have been premier in the example, but they were in no way frowned upon. Bible writings are rich in the contributions and leadership and sacrifices of women. Therefore, this is not in any manner a discourse on the inferiority of women.

The best love that a man can show a woman and children is to guide them in the knowledge and relationship of God.

A common myth in the family and even in society is that a woman is to submit to a man. Not so. God has stated throughout the Word that a wife is to submit to her own husband as unto God (Ephesians 5:22). Never have I read that a woman is to submit to a man because of gender. There are many examples of a woman submitting to a man because of the authority position that God has placed him in. Therefore, the generic and across the board submission theory is in total error of God's intended purpose for mankind.

We are not to be lone rangers in society, nor to be dictators over the gems that God has placed in our care.

The order of the household is man, the husband and father, woman, the wife and helper, and children the combined godly seed that are to continue the destiny of God for mankind. We are not to be lone rangers in society, nor to be dictators over the gems that God has placed in our care. The best love that a man can show a woman and children is to guide them in the knowledge and relationship of God. That is the ultimate display of love. And, that will also be the ultimate sacrifice made. For it is often a very difficult task trying to attempt to live your life as God has ordained while showing others the way. Yet, we do this through the grace of God and our desire to mirror Him in this earth. Selah.

When a man is promiscuous, and it has happened even in the church, he is considered as "being a man".

Society sets many mixed standards for humanity. First of all, society somehow places one gender above another; usually the masculine gender. An example would be in the early American culture. A woman was not considered to be equal with a man, and thus not able to be considered in the foundation of America. Throughout history, the rights of women have been championed on many fronts. Now, in America, a woman is to have equal rights and opportunities as a man, even though this is not always the case. There can always be found situations where even though laws are passed and instituted, women can still be hindered because of a warped mindset of manhood. Sadly, there are those that would use the Word of God to justify this false doctrine.

Nothing is worse than trying to show your worthiness to be a man by aggressive, uncompassionate, and coarse behavior and actions.

We can also look at those examples that we have witnessed within the last five or so decades. When a man is promiscuous, and it has happened even in the church, he is considered as "being a man". But, let the women behave in the same way and she is labeled horrible things because she given a much higher standard than man. This is not to be so. God stated in Galatians 3:28:

> *There is neither Jew nor Greek, there is neither slave nor free, there is neither male nor female; for you are all one in Christ Jesus.*

This same standard of holiness is held high for both genders. And, as being the earthly example of our heavenly Father, what are we showing to those who are looking for Him in us?

As society distorts manhood, we are often measured by our possessions and accomplishments. Nothing is worse than trying to show your worthiness to be a man by aggressive, uncompassionate, and coarse behavior and actions. Our

Source is not any of these actions. How is it that we can think that we are like Him with such flaws?

As I understand and view His character toward us, I can only worship. God has been very loving to the point of already providing a sacrifice ahead of time to reconcile us back to Him in eternity. Revelation 13:8 KJV gives us a glimpse of how in eternity, God already made provision for us.

> *All who dwell on the earth will worship him, whose names have not been written in the Book of Life of the Lamb slain from the foundation of the world.*

This is a loving glimpse of knowing those who have been placed in your life. We are to have a plan already in place for those who fall short just as God had for us. It will be a sad commentary if we make it up as we go along as we so often do. I did. Only with proper Biblical instruction did I begin to get a clue as to what was required and even possible for me as a man. As men, we are to be very familiar with those who God has trusted us to guide; whether they are by marriage, biological, social or spiritual. There have been and will continue to be failures. But, we serve a God of multiple chances, not just second chances. We have to already acknowledge the slain Lamb for any shortcoming that these individuals possess. After all, before we were in the physical realm, we were covered. Therefore, society can never dictate the character, love and faithfulness of God.

Reflection

What do you consider the foundational unit of the earth or community and why?

What can you do to strengthen the Biblical foundational community even if not everyone is Christian?

How can you guide those under this community unit in the ways of God?

The Power of Your Will

I find it interesting that in our formation as man, God never constructed our will that it would be subservient. It was something that we personally had control over. This is the proverbial theological and philosophical rock that is so heavy that even God can't lift it. I have had many come to me with this "philosophical" question in the attempt to trap me in not knowing how to answer it. This is the reason that a disciple must know when to answer an person, when to allow the Holy Spirit to answer them through you and when to just tell the person that they are making as much sense as a screen door on a submarine.

In the model prayer that Jesus gave the disciples He said to pray that the Father's will be done, on earth just as it was in heaven. In addition, Jesus even voiced the command for the Father's will to be done while in the Garden of Gethsemane. So, this "will" is something to be reckoned with. It is not something that is to be dismissed.

It is my thought process that we all have the same power in our will but utilize it differently.

We hear someone say that he or she is strong willed. What is that really saying? Are we any stronger in our will that what God has already given us? I beg to differ. It is my thought process that we all have the same power in our will but utilize it differently. I liken this to all of us having a live artillery shell. It has the same dimensions, possibilities and purpose. Yet, there are those who will modify it either for good or bad. But, the initial presentation was for a live artillery round to be used in a military action and not as a passive paperweight.

We as men must understand that our will is not alone.

God gave us our will, but to be used to do His will. He did not make us robots or clones. We are created in His image; with a will. We as men must understand that our will is not alone. It is accompanied by four other companions; mind, intellect, imagination and emotions. This in effect makes up our soul or *psuche* which is the Greek word.

I picture this in a sense as the five-fold ascension or ministry gifts that are listed in Ephesians 4:11 (wow, I gave another location away). But, in this passage we are told that there are five gifts of ministry. These are the ascension gifts for the perfecting of the Body of Christ. I do beg to differ somewhat, but that is just me. Now, please don't go and argue with every Christian you see about what I am about to present.

Various translations have worth in my opinion as long as you can go to the original language.

Scripture is not by any private interpretation. But, in the passage the order is listed as apostle, prophet, evangelist, pastor and teacher. Again, I like to challenge people not as one to cause disruption, but to give thought to a possibility. Very possibly we have been told something that we erroneously or incompletely repeated.

I love looking into the original language to see what has been said. I do this because there are those who ascribe to translations that I have no idea how they accept. And, there are those who will put you in hell if they could because you won't read King James Version only. I'm not here to tell you what you personally need to study. Various translations have worth in my opinion as long as you can go to the original language for clarity and evaluation. This is the case with the five-fold ministry.

The teacher must be either an apostolic, prophetic, evangelistic or pastoral teacher.

I noticed that apostle, prophet, evangelist and pastor were on one side of the word which represents our word for and in the Greek language: *kai*. Then there is the same root for the words for pastor and teacher. Could it be that even though there are five gifts listed that we cannot operate in such ascension or leadership ministry unless we are operating simultaneously in two gifts? Now, I offer this though because the only gift that cannot operate along with this method is that of a teacher. An apostle must also be able to teach. A prophet must be also a teacher. An evangelist must be a teacher. And, a pastor surely must be able to teach. But, a teacher can't teach themselves. They cannot be a teacher teacher. The teacher must be either an apostolic, prophetic, evangelistic or pastoral teacher. This balances the work of edifying and equipping the saints.

I will my intellect to reflect God.

So, this view is where I return to the will. Our will must also be able to be applied to the other aspects of our soul; mind, imagination, intellect and emotions. We must ensure that God's "will" be done over ours. This is accomplished by using our will to ensure our mind, imagination, intellect and emotions remain Godly. Where I draw this similarity, others will not. And, they will want to fight me about it if they could; perhaps not physically. In essence what I am saying is that I will my mind to be godly. I will my emotions to be godly. I will my intellect to reflect God. I will my imaginations to be godly. I will allow His will to be done on earth as in heaven. So, this will be a willful action.

God gives us free will, but not freedom of choice.

This brings me to the conclusion of the power of our will. God gave us a will. We were not restricted in the use and application of it. We willed ourselves to be in accordance with His directives in the Garden. Then we willed our own eviction through sinful choices. I say choices because it was more than one choice that caused us to be evicted. Now, this may be a kicker for some. And, I am in no way stating that what my thought pattern is should be yours. But, my will is in essence free to make the choice.

He set before us death and life.

God gives us free will, but not freedom of choice. I can hear many that want to address this. We have free will to choose; the ability to choose. Yet, God tells us what to choose since our prayer is for His will to be done on earth as in heaven. He set before us death and life. Then He explicitly said to choose life. Process that same scenario as this. You are sitting in a multiple-choice examination. The professor sets a series of answers in front of you. Yet, you must choose the answer the professor has told you to choose. Only then will you receive the reward for the answer; a good grade. Yet that same professor will not stand over you and tell you that you had better let him choose your answer. This is how our Lord is. He will give you the choices and then will tell you through lectures/sermons/meditations which one is the right answer. But, He will not "make" you choose the right one. He only hopes that we will because He has told you the right answers.

So in essence, our will is one of the most powerful things on earth. Our will can bring God into the earth or limit His ability. Our will can give us life or death. Our will can bring us happiness or turmoil. And, our will shapes the world in which we live. Our will needs to be in line with His will. Or else we will not be full in Christ. Selah.

Reflection

Do you know when to answer a person that is attempting to ridicule your faith by asking questions concerning your will? (Christians should not be asking this)

How many times have you not allowed God to move the rock of your will?

Have you surrendered all of your intellect, imagination, emotions, mind, and will (the complete essence of your soul) over to Jesus?

The Bull of a Man

Men, we are often referred to as bull headed, stubborn, strong as an ox and many other things. How about we begin to turn this thing around and apply something to these sometimes true analogies? The bull was an animal that is considered clean according to the Mosaic Law. Since it was a clean animal then there must have been certain characteristics concerning it. One of the characteristics is that it had to have a parted hoof or a split hoof such as a cow, sheep, goat or deer.

The hoof doesn't have many nerves in it.

We can understand how we are to stand by looking at this first aspect of the split hoof on the bull. As a man, we are to be able to stand in two dimensions; natural and spiritual. I would even expand this analogy to other dual stances too such as family and society, religious and governmental. And, this list could go on. But, the split hoof gives us a thought of where we should place our footing so to speak. I mean it is constantly said that we are what we eat, right? So, we are this animal that must have sure footing in two places simultaneously.

That hoof also says that our footing is not easily wounded to be moved such as a paw or toes. The hoof doesn't have many nerves in it. Therefore, it is harder to cause pain in the hoof as it is in the animal's paw or on your toes. So, our footing is firmer with less pain once we place it in the right place. With the hoof we can "dig in" better to progress. It has a design to dig into the earth in order to pull loads or propel the body. This is what is needed for us to sometimes pull a load much bigger than our own. We need to dig into the ground to become mobile and sure. So, are you beginning to feel better about our bull analogies now? I am.

We then begin to "chew" it again thereby extracting more nutrients from it.

Chewing the cud can be a gross image when you look at a bull. He has this mouth full of green stuff or hay and is just chewing. Such table manners already get us in trouble. But, yet we will continue supplanting this derogatory reference to us. Let's chew some cud. Cud is regurgitated food. It's that simple. So, let's regurgitate our food which is the Word of God. We eat of the Bread of Life, regurgitate it and eat it again. This is called meditation to us (not to the bull certainly). We hear the word initially and then digest that immediate nutrition from it. In times to come, we hear that same word again as we bring it back to our remembrance; regurgitate it. We then begin to "chew" it again thereby extracting more nutrients from it. Now, the bull has four stomachs! So, this is a lot of regurgitation (meditation) before that meal/sermon/teaching is moved on from. It still never leaves our system fully because of the digestion factor.

> ***It's a sad commentary for so many Christians to be in such an uproar about a movie as if we are holding Hollywood to a standard of Biblical soundness.***

How often is it that we leave church after hearing a sermon and that's it? Sadly, this how most Christians, not just men approach feasting upon the Word of God. The pastor preaches the Word and then people hear it on the way out the door. There is no regurgitation of it ever. It's on to the next Sunday attendance requirement. It is this mentality that causes us to be such non-light to the world. We can't carry the light because we don't embrace the light. As a quick sidebar I would like to give an example of light that is ineffective.

> ***If we do not carry the presence and power of God, there can be no release of Him in any fashion.***

I recently viewed a movie from Hollywood: Noah. While there many things that a theologian or even a studious Christian would question, the movie to me was a good movie! Notice I said it was a good movie. I did not say that it was theologically sound and that I would bank my salvation on the movie, the director or anything else. It's a sad commentary for so many Christians to be in such an uproar about a movie as if we are holding Hollywood to a standard of Biblical soundness. Get real. The movie had great special effects and action. I'll stop it there. But, what I saw that amazed me were the watchers; these mythical angels that had somehow been doomed to be hideous rock creatures with attitudes toward all humans. When the 'creator' wasn't mad at them anymore and allowed them to return to wherever they came from, immediately this 'light' burst forth from their inner being to be whisked away. This is the same light that we are to have as Christians. However, we can't release what we don't carry! If we do not carry the presence and power of God, there can be no release of Him in any fashion. The Holy Spirit must be in us in order to come out of us. I am not speaking of the indwelling of the Holy Spirit that occurs when we accept Christ as Lord and Savior. I am speaking of the Baptism of the Holy Spirit that gives us this *dunamis* power that is endowed from on high. This is the power that is needed to perform miracles, cast out demons, change natural events and even navigate past temptation for a changed life.

> ***Every time there is a release of the Word of God we chew it, swallow it and then walk away.***

So, I speak this because these 'watchers' had the power, but it was locked up. This is the case with many of us. As men, we have the power. But, we don't know how to use it or how we need to use it. We have all of this light/Word of God locked up in us with self-imposed rocks holding it in. Every time there is a release of the Word of God we chew it, swallow it and then walk away. That's the end of it. We in essence become a 'watcher'; power in us, but a rocky existence. I have three words for this: simple, sad and stupid. Why would we have the power to blast a mountain, obtain precious stones to become financially ultra-wealthy and only pick up pine cones to hopefully find seeds? It makes no sense to me. Yet, we do it.

We should maintain dominion everywhere.

So, let's return to the chewing of the cud. The bull has four stomachs. Four is representative of dominion and the corners of the earth. We are to have 'digestion/meditation' of all areas of the earth. Our dominion should never be limited to the space in front of our hands. We should maintain dominion everywhere. This is why there should be a constant "chewing of the cud" in order to apply that same meal to every situation whether it be in church, at work, at home or just while traveling. The stomach of digestion changes to meet different scenarios. To revisit the split hoof, we are standing in two different dimensions simultaneously. Therefore, we should constantly bring up the precious "chewing" to extract more spiritual nutrients from it for the scenario at hand.

Before long you will be speaking and even preaching this same word with your own flavor of course.

Each 'stomach' of the bull has a special digestive ability. The initial stomach is the one that is the immediate intake. It named the *rumen* stomach. It is here where a lot is taken in. It is in this stage that the bull chews on what he has ingested for many times before it is moved on. This is where we as men need to truly give heed to. We need to chew, regurgitate, chew again and the continue the process until we have reduced the meal of the Word of God into smaller more digestible pieces to move on to the next phase of our growth. But, again, this is the place where we need to continuously process what we have received. We do this by listening to that same word over and over, studying it in our private meditation time and even discussing it among people. Before long you will be speaking and even preaching this same word with your own flavor of course.

As with anything you will sometimes have things in your meal that doesn't need to be there. This is the purpose of the second stomach; the *reticulum*. It is here that things that should not have been eaten such as sticks, pieces of wire or anything that may harm the bull becomes trapped. Yet, it is also in this area that the meal that is to be digested receives even more attention; more digestive enzymes to break it down further. In relation to what has heard this is where you not only go over the notes, assuming there were notes taken, but also dig into background of the pericope of Scripture, certain words, customs that are being portrayed and a host of other things. It is at this point where I am digging so deeply into the original language or the intended example of the historical custom until I can get lost for hours.

It is here that often you will take a serious break to experience a series of "Selah" moments.

The third stomach, the *omasum*, is a place with many folds to filter the food while squeezing out any water that remains in it. It further digests the food making it possible to break down the 'cud' even further. It is here where we are to see how this passage or sermon relates to another that we have heard. We are looking to connect this passage with another passage. It is here that often you will take a serious break to experience a series of "Selah" moments. This is a place where some things come together that you may have heard and pondered from the past. It's a wonderful place. The 'ah ha' moments here can be so wonderful until there is a marked response and expression. I have an expression of yelling out when a rhema hits me. My wife looks at me like the cow looking at a new gate; confused. By now I would think she is used to me. It's a wonderful place to be when that one thing bombards your spirit and mind simultaneously.

It is a point of extraction.

The final stomach for our spiritual anatomy of the bull is the *abomasum*. This is where the process is finished, sending those things needed for the moment to the body while discarding the others. It is a point of extraction. We extract what is needed while releasing the rest. In the physical anatomy of a bull, this would be the place of elimination. This is not so in the spirit realm. What is not needed it stored in a 'place' to begin the process again when needed.

… I cannot relay anything to you unless I have been taught and practice the same.

Now, at this point you may be heralding my superior and thorough veterinary and zoological training. If so, I cannot accept your accolades. I only received the message from God through my pastor and began the digestion process through my 'four stomachs' being a bull figure. My pastor was the one who presented this information. I received it and even dug a tad more on certain areas. But, he initially fed me this 'cud' for me to chew on. And, I have been doing this for quite some time with this very same message. So, my brothers you see that I cannot relay anything to you unless I have been taught and practice the same. Don't chew the fat. Chew the cud. Selah…

Reflection

How often do you chew the "cud" of the Word?

Can you regurgitate and re-digest a sermon or word received in the past to make it applicable to today? And, how far in the past is your cud?

Can you identify what aspect of the word received that you didn't initially digest that possibly you should have?

Where Did You Become Missing?

In the military there is a gathering called a formation in which every person is to be present and accounted for. Disciplinary action, reassignments and change of occupations occurred because a military soldier or sailor "missed formation". Could it be that we as men have missed many formations and therefore allowed the enemy to reassign us without the authorization of God? It is within the musings such as this where we have to take inventory of our own formations that were missed. Now, we have to formulate a plan as to either return to position or maintain the disconnection of which we have been part of.

If we wish to "blame" people, places and things for the place where we are at this present moment, we become foolish and choose death.

Most likely there will be many different points of missing our formation that we can identify. I cannot and would never dare speak to the formation that is missed for another man without permission. However, in my own life I have identified many missed formations. Again, it's up to us how we adjust or "recover" for such missed necessities. The moment we identify a point and then dwell in it, we become stagnant and die. There is no other way to put it. If we wish to "blame" people, places and things for the place where we are at this present moment, we become foolish and choose death.

Most often the first missed formation is a generational formation.

I spoke to a dear brother about my intention to become transparent with brothers within a group. He rebuked me stating that someone may tell my past. That is my intention, to have my past told; by me! Who can tell it better than you? This way there is no secret. But, in telling past events or pains it would not be to justify where I am, but to truly give a testimony to God's power and majesty in waiting for me to accept Him. The main purpose would be to alert those that are looking into the past for missed formations and what signs to recognize them by. This way we as men could truly be our brother's keeper in assisting others to recognize their own missed formations and realign ourselves into position to ensure many timely formations.

There has to be a point of one looking in the mirror, acknowledging the sins of the fathers and vowing through the grace of God to change direction.

Most often the first missed formation is a generational formation. It has been missed well before you arrived on earth via your mother's womb. This may be a societal norm that was developed through historical ignorance or injustice. It may even have a religious overtone in order to appear as a righteous action. However, it is a missed formation. And, it must be corrected. Otherwise the generational curse and absence will be perpetual.

There has to be a point of one looking in the mirror, acknowledging the sins of the fathers and vowing through the grace of God to change direction.

There was a time when I would just reminisce concerning what could have been only if I had been given proper guidance. Well, the Lord had to rebuke me concerning my subconscious questioning of His will and purpose for my life. This is exactly what we are doing when we want to think "if only" thoughts. We are actually saying, "God, if only You had done better…" In times like this, we are really saying that we had a better plan even though we did not know it at the time the existence of any plan. This is ludicrous thinking; right? But, this is what our actions dictate!

I was to be the one that stood in the gap of connection to God's purpose and truth for my descendants.

It was during one of these historical mental excursions when I realized that I am the catalyst for the change in this missed formation. I was to be the one that stood in the gap of connection to God's purpose and truth for my descendants. Whether or not they would accept it was not the issue. My purpose was to acknowledge, intercede and live as the example of one that takes the position of change. It was then that I began to understand that we are never far from change. Our only difficulty is obeying what God said and not what we were inadvertently taught. And, in all honesty, I actually used to question what I was taught because it seemed bizarre in many instances or far from the mere limited understanding of God as I had.

Our next formation that is missed concerns Biblical formation. Somehow as the development of the church progressed in time, various doctrines slipped in unaware. Within these trespasses were hidden religious practices that either held no value according to the Bible or were warped in their interpretation of certain passages to support a belief or action in order to solidify some aspect of control. The misrepresentation of Biblical truth was wrapped in societal practices. The most common misrepresentation of Biblical truth concerned submission. While submission was forced upon women with partial Scriptural application and preaching, men were not being forthright in what God presented to us for action. Not only did we not study the Word in order to gain proper knowledge that would lead to revelation, application and then illumination, but we also placed others on pedestals because of our slothfulness.

Once the man or woman (did I say that?) of God preaches, teaches or prophesies a word from God to us, it is our responsibility as men to thoroughly research the spoken word, not to question them, but to gain a further understanding of what was given and its validity or accuracy. In this manner we can now "re" present it to our family, community and relatives.

But, we cannot do this unless we are first partakers of the fruit. So we must be accounted for in the formation of Biblical truth.

There is also a missed formation of silence. My man of God spoke once on the vocabulary of silence. This is tantamount to humility and the recognition of conflict but choosing not to participate in it. Too often a man will herald past experiences and even exploits to justify a present existence. The moment this happens we step out of the vocabulary of silence and step into a boisterous celebration of often ungodly actions and existence. We begin to shape our dysfunction with past dysfunctional memories and justification. While I can tell "some" instances of my past actions in a comedic way, I preface it by saying that I am in NO way proud of it.

We must be silent and reverential to God's communication with us through His word, His messenger and His people.

Recently I returned to a place that I was stationed. At the time I only knew to "go there" and just hear from God. I did. What He showed me was how I was kept by Him in so many ways! I had never understood why I was there as much as I did years after being there. As I traveled all of the "stops" in my life there in the area, I realized that each step while allowed by God was for my development to bring me to a place of today. I even went to my apartment in the area to see it run down and overgrown yet occupied. It was in no way the serene escape from military life (and dysfunctional actions) that I once knew. A silence fell upon me in such a way as to not celebrate but grieve how we as men can speak or allow so much noise and overlook the hand of God on our lives. We must be silent and reverential to God's communication with us through His word, His messenger and His people. Yet, our refusal to be silent and still will negate His message coming to us for various reasons. This is why we must be present in the formation of stillness.

When mentoring anyone, I always ask of their relationship with their father.

As many missed formations can be identified, I will only mention a few to allow us to do extensive soul searching to identify formations that have been missed and not necessarily listed here. This will bring us to the final mentioned formation for this communication: the missed formation of fatherhood. When mentoring anyone, I always ask of their relationship with their father. Why? I ask this because until that relationship is settled, growth will be stunted. This is where many of us miss our formation because of the relationship we have had or don't have with our father.

The missed formation of paternal relationship can cause many things. It will inadvertently cause competition if we do not have a secure relationship or a resolved understanding of a lacking or failed relationship with our father. A dear friend of mine once explained how he was raised by a teenage mother with no father present. He went on to explain how this bothered him in years to come. This was until he realized at age thirty that his father was not coming home to play ball with him. So, he finally "left off of the porch" and began to live as God intended.

Men become "Mamma's boys" and often will overcompensate for the missed relationship or absence of the father.

How many times do we as men stay "on the porch" of life because we secretly despise the one that we are to honor? I have stated before that honor and cherish have two distinct definitions. And, as a man faces the relationship or lack of one with his father certain behaviors disappear that are detrimental; competition, anger, manipulation and overachievement. Anger is nothing more than masking a known but not acknowledged insecurity that is acted out in competition. This is all because we have missed the accountability formation for our father issues. By, the way this spills over into our understanding of God the Father. We paint Him as being askew from His character; the epitome of love.

What is presented and accepted as being a hard or strong man is often the result and camouflage of being scared and weak.

It is times like this when a substitution is made. Men become "Mamma's boys" and often will overcompensate for the missed relationship or absence of the father. This manifests in the competitive and combative spirit toward other men and also the overprotectiveness and rescue of women. To be honest, this can be the spirit of lesbianism in which we attempt to be something of a man that we are not because of a pain concerning a man; the absence or dysfunction of the father. What is presented and accepted as being a hard or strong man is often the result and camouflage of being hurt, scared and weak. Yet, if we connect to one another we can carry one another through this situation concerning our transformation. We all have some form of missing the formation of the father issue in our lives. Only when we get within our own psyche and identify our need for transparency will we be delivered from the uncertainty of father.

Reflection

Can you articulate without pain or bitterness the relationship with your father? Have you forgiven his shortcomings or absence? Are they resolved within you?

Are you a "mamma's boy" in which areas of insecurity and emptiness hide behind the guise of manhood?

Can you identify areas of missed formations in your life in a truthful manner to another brother?

My God, My Pastor and Me
(The Launch into the Atmosphere of Life)

In conclusion, we must begin an order that will align us in order to properly be guided and covered. While many have erred for various reasons in the individual order of God for a man which is beneficial to a man and his life, we must align ourselves with the proper order. This order is the foundational relational order that must be established in order to ensure that we as men don't become missing in God.

First of all, we must understand that God is first in our lives. There is no other person that is to have preeminence in our lives except God. This is tantamount for us to understand our origin in Him prior to arrival to the earth realm. This enables us to understand our source. It is in Him that we live, move and have our being. In order for Him to be first, He must be made first by acceptance of the Sacrifice rejoining us to Him; His Son Christ Jesus. I speak to anyone who has not accepted Christ as your Lord and Savior to do so now. Nothing spooky is to befall you. Simply pray to Him. He hears. A simple prayer of:

> *"Lord, I am in need of your Son Jesus as my Lord and Savior. Your Word states and You said that it is true since you cannot lie that if I confess Jesus as Lord with my mouth and believe in my heart that I am saved. Therefore, I believe already in my heart which is causing me to confess into the atmosphere with my mouth that Jesus is my Lord and Savior. Therefore, I am saved according to the promises that you have given me and many before me. Now, I ask that your Holy Spirit would guide me to where I must go to learn more of you and be covered by a loving pastor. I ask this in the name of Jesus. Amen."*

Now, according to His promises you are saved. This is the first part of the transition. You have now connected to God in order to move to the next phase.

The next phase you must connect to is a man or woman of God; a personal pastor with whom can guide and teach you. While this may not be in a one on one setting, there must be a connection. A congregation is nothing more than a number of individuals all needing the same thing as you; covering and guidance. Therefore, it is good for brothers to be a viable part of a Bible believing and teaching congregation headed by your own personal pastor who will impart into your life. Don't be fooled by the enemy thinking you can receive the same at home. You can't.

Everything has a function and position.

The Body of Christ is likened as an organism not an organization. Therefore, an organism can live without a member. But, the member can't live without the organism. In an organization, you may interchange all the people in the positions you are assigned. However, in the organism you cannot take a toenail and make it a brain nor take a knee and make it a heart. Everything has a function and position. The same is of you my brother in the Body of Christ and local congregation. You have a specific assigned of God function. Now, you must connect to do it.

Do not despise the person of God that is assigned to lead you.

Your pastor gives a report to the Lord concerning you while hearing some things concerning you from the Lord to help you maneuver while on earth. I am not in any fashion stating that the only way you will hear God is from your pastor. But, I would truly think that the majority of time he speaks in the form of teaching a Bible study, a sermon or even in private conversation you will receive some form of communication from his lips to your spirit. Do not despise the person of God that is assigned to lead you.

It is also your responsibility to develop, maintain and strengthen your relationship with the Lord. If you are in a relationship with your wife, you do not marry her then leave and never speak to her again. We all would question whether or not you are married. You marry her during the wedding. After that begins the growth and increased relational intimacy of the marriage. It is very similar with God. When you are saved, you will begin to search him out. He will play hide and seek with you. He will allow you to find Him then go to another place for you to find Him in the new place. It's a wonderful thing! It never gets boring! In this development of relationship and increased intimacy all areas of your life will blossom.

It is proper in this instance to be the first partaker of the fruit that you receive.

Now come the final aspect; ME. With all the things that God shows us, it is our responsibility to implement what is given to us. We are to be the first partakers of the meal He serves whether through His word, through prophetic utterance or a *rhema* that is spoken into the atmosphere and caught in our spirit. Remember, a starving cook is a fool. You are to taste firsthand to see the goodness of what God is speaking and serving from whatever source before you attempt to serve it to another. It is proper in this instance to be the first partaker of the fruit that you receive. All of this points to the subject of me. I am the one that must desire to change. I am the one that must implement the change. I am the one that must continue maintaining after the change. This is one time when the "I" factor is desirable; when I am the focus of the change.

And when it is all in line it is God, then my pastor, then me that must maintain this line of communication. God will never stop speaking to us. How He chooses to do so will be the only variable. My pastor is assigned to guide, protect and provide spiritual food for me. And, I must be committed to change, growth, development and determination to become more like Christ. I am not to be the missing man in the formation. I will be in formation to move as a unit toward all that God has intended. I am present and accounted for. Selah…

NOTES FOR MEDITATION AND CONTEMPLATION

www.ingramcontent.com/pod-product-compliance
Lightning Source LLC
Chambersburg PA
CBHW032038290426
44110CB00012B/852